UNFORGET
LEADERSHIP

7 PRINCIPLES
for
Leading, Learning, & Living

SHERRY YELLIN, PHD

Publisher's Cataloging-In-Publication Data
(Prepared by The Donohue Group, Inc.)

Names: Yellin, Sherry, author.
Title: Unforgettable leadership : 7 principles for leading, learning, & living / Sherry Yellin, PhD.
Description: [Farmersville, Texas] : [Learning Connection, LLC], [2019] | Includes bibliographical references.
Identifiers: ISBN 9781733502009
Subjects: LCSH: Leadership--Psychological aspects. | Brain--Psychophysiology. | Learning, Psychology of. | Psychology, Industrial. | Neuroscience.
Classification: LCC BF637.L4 Y45 2019 | DDC 158.4--dc23

Library of Congress Control Number: 2018914861
ISBN: 9781733502009

To the great Creator

"Do not be conformed to this world but be transformed by the renewing of your mind."

Romans 12:2

Acknowledgement

Perhaps the most humbling and daunting part of this project comes now—acknowledging and honoring those who have made so many moments in my life unforgettable. These are the people on my journey who created a CRANIUM culture for me so that I could fail safely and soar boldly.

Thank you to the people who know me best and love me anyway. Nolan and Callie, you are adventurous, free-spirited sojourners down roads we never expected but navigated with triumph. Life with the two of you is never boring, and I would not have it any other way; my love for you both has no boundaries! Lance Blakley, thank you for asking and for every moment since. Lisa Strickland, you always believed in and stood with me. You are my rock and my hero. To my parents, LeRoy and Linda Willis, thank you for loving me and filling in the gap in a thousand ways. And to my squad, you are the best friends anyone could have.

Serendipity—expecting one thing and gaining so much more—is a theme that runs throughout my life. Thank you to those who have come into my life unexpectedly and changed me forever. Hillary Evans and Becca Haskell, keep impacting the world. Daniel Bender, thank you for keeping the vision and pushing me to finish. Susan Dawson-O'Brien, a brilliant editor, you were divinely appointed to help me in completing this project. And Kata Schuyler, thank you for getting me across the finish line.

My sincere gratitude goes out to the people who have helped me develop professionally in ways I couldn't have imagined. Dr. Dick Fulkerson, thank you for giving me an F because you knew I could achieve more. Kathy Price, you saw the potential in me when I didn't see it in myself. Kathy Jones, you are one of the greatest leaders I've ever known. Chris Kenney, I'm so grateful you helped me renovate my brain. And Mina Brown, thank you for introducing me to the power of coaching.

To the thousands of people who have participated in my workshops, retreats, and coaching over the years, thank you for challenging me; sharing your thoughts, victories and struggles; staying vulnerable; and allowing me to be a part of your development. Most of all, thank you for coming back from break!

To all my clients over the years who trusted me to come into their organizations, their schools, their churches, their homes, know that I never take that trust for granted, and I am grateful for the opportunity to serve each and every one of you.

And finally, a special thanks to you, my reader. Follow your calling.

Contents

Preface

A lot of things in life are memorable...very few are unforgettable.

I often begin my workshops by having the participants share "unforgettable" stories: the greatest leader they have had the privilege of knowing personally; that one presentation, teacher, or learning experience they remember, though they've sat through thousands of hours of lectures; that "no-matter-what" moment in their lives when—no matter what—they accomplished what they set out to do.

Of course, "unforgettable" also applies to those moments in our careers and in our lives that are not-so-positive and uplifting: the person who, in our experience, deserves the "worst boss" award; the endless hours of torture-by-lecture we've all endured; those moments in our personal lives we may want to erase but which, nevertheless, have helped shape who we are.

In a world of memorable, these are the experiences, the beautiful and the tragic, that are unforgettable.

This book is not about the negative unforgettables that set us back, knock us down, and hinder us from becoming our best selves. This book is about creating positive unforgettables by which to lead, live, and learn:

- Unforgettable leadership
- Unforgettable cultures
- Unforgettable results

This book is about a quest to create environments on purpose and with intention—for ourselves and for those we influence—where we can become our best selves, live our best lives, and leave our best legacies.

All we have to do is lead, live, and learn the way the brain works best. And the best news? It doesn't have to be hard.

CRANIUM Cultures

I f you take away nothing else from this book, know this: when we create cultures based on how the brain works best, unforgettable magic happens in our leadership, in our learning, and in our lives. Why, then, aren't we doing it?

One fact about the brain is it craves to know "why." To our brain, most things have very little meaning or impact unless we get the "why" behind the "how." The importance of knowing the "why" applies to leadership decisions, math concepts, grammar and punctuation, spiritual issues, weight loss, budgeting, career choices, child discipline, and even writing this book. You get the idea.

The "why" behind this book has been building for more than two decades as I've worked with thousands of leaders who serve in various capacities around the world.

My original "why" was to start a revolution—that is, until I read Jon Acuff, who, in his book *Start*, tells readers we should never begin a book by stating we want to start a revolution. Bummer. But starting one still seems so appropriate.

A revolution, according to Merriam-Webster, is a sudden, extreme, or complete change in the way people live, work...and think.

Hmmm. I don't see many revolutions going on around me when it comes to leading, learning, and living the way the brain works best. Yet I believe wholeheartedly that we need one. Now.

The revolution I want to see is for leaders—whether they call themselves VPs, managers, parents, teachers, or influencers—to embrace the belief that if we create a culture aligned with how the brain works best, all of the unforgettable results we crave will naturally occur.

Think about this: when was the last time you were in an environment (used interchangeably in this book with the word culture) where there was high trust, creativity, innovation, excellent communication, engagement, and acceptance at work, school, home, or other venue of life? I'm guessing it was also an environment enjoying high performance and impressive results with fewer challenges. (No surprise there.)

The reason for the stellar outcomes was because you were in a brain-friendly environment, or as I call it, a CRANIUM culture. But what exactly made that situation brain-compatible? How does that happen? And how can we create another one?

Now contemplate this: think about the last time you were in an environment (culture) at work, school, home, or other venue of life where there was distrust, complaining, whining, cynicism, blaming, disengagement, and apathy. My guess is it was also a culture that tolerated mediocre performance with marginal results and unnecessary problems. (Again, not surprising.) The reason for the poor outcomes was because you were in a brain-antagonistic environment, or an anti-CRANIUM culture. But what made that situation brain-antagonistic? How does that happen? And how can we prevent or change that?

These questions can be answered when we explore the seven principles of a CRANIUM culture.

A CRANIUM culture is one that caters to the very equipment we are all striving to maximize—the brain. The brain is where the magic happens, and the brain is what fuels innovation, engagement, commitment, performance, and relationships. When the culture is aligned with how the brain works best, our desired results are easy to attain. When the culture is not aligned with how the brain works best, we will never get what we seek.

Take the analogy of a plant. When we create the perfect environment for a particular plant to grow, intentionally having the moisture, soil, temperature, sunlight, and so forth on point for that plant, it naturally grows and flourishes, and the results are astonishing. (No mystery there.) We achieved the best result because the plant was growing in an environment perfectly suited to make it flourish. The results came easily because attention was given to creating the right environment.

The same holds true for the brain. When we give attention to creating a culture aligned with how it works best, we see it flourish.

Creating an inviting culture isn't difficult. Say you are a university professor whose goal is to teach an online class; you need the right technology, right? You also need to know a few things about how the learning technology works. Now, if you are a NASCAR driver, and your goal is to win a race, you also need the right technology. Additionally, you need to know a few things about how a race car's technology works. Or, if you are a NASA scientist, and your goal is to get a human to the moon, you again need the right technology. You also need to know a few things about how space travel technology works. See the pattern?

So, what if you are a leader and your goal is to create a culture of results such as trust, ownership, engagement, communication, and innovation? You need the right technology. And you need to know a few things about how it works.

In the same way the right technology helps professors, race car drivers, and scientists achieve their goals, the brain is the technology that helps leaders who aspire to grow themselves, create healthy, productive cultures, and develop other leaders. So they must utilize their technology (the brain) to get the desired results, just like teaching a great class, winning a race, or accomplishing a mission.

Over my 20+ years of working in a variety of settings, my suspicions have proven true. The brain—not a tablet, smartphone, or computer—is the most important technology we have had (or ever will). It is the most crucial piece of equipment in our workplaces, in our homes, and in our classrooms. Knowing the principles behind how it works can change performance, learning, and lives.

The brain is what will set nations apart, allow people of all ages to reach their full potential, enable workplaces to be innovative and productive, and create rich, safe, loving homes. The brain is also what allows that professor with the online class to communicate effectively; that race car driver to find the discipline, focus, and courage to win the race; and that scientist to have the grit and determination to accomplish the mission. The brain is the center of all things. It is by far the most important technology on the planet.

Given the importance of this greatest piece of technology and witnessing the powerful results achieved when we align with how it works, I'm baffled at how much we know about our mobile phones but how little we know about our brains. I often wonder why we take such precaution when handling our high-tech devices and have so little regard for the way we take care of our brains. But more on that later.

While everyone benefits from knowing how to apply the basics of how the brain learns best, there is one audience for whom this information will have the greatest impact.

Unforgettable Leadership

They are a group of people who can transform cultures in all settings—home, work, school, and community. They must be equipped with knowledge about the brain and armed with practical ways to implement that knowledge. Who are they? Those who call themselves "leaders."

So who is a leader? Defining this can seem like a monumental task requiring complicated analysis. Since the beginning of time, great minds have attempted to bring clarity to this elusive term. Literally thousands of books have been written in the attempt to define who a leader is, what a leader does, how a leader looks, and so forth. It is really messy stuff.

When leaders better understand the brain, they have an edge. They create brain-friendly cultures, environments where the brain is naturally at its best. The result? Unforgettable relationships. Unforgettable cultures. Unforgettable performance. Unforgettable lives. The good news? It doesn't have to be hard.

Leadership has little to do with age, title, gender, or salary. A leader is simply someone who has a different mindset.

In essence, leaders are eternal learners and teachers. They are constantly curious, hungry to learn, and eager to grow and evolve, but not solely for their own personal gain. Their driving motivation is to assist others to also grow and evolve. As my good friend and colleague, Veronica Cochran of L.I.F.E. Concepts, says, "A leader is someone dedicated to developing other leaders."

If that's you, thank you for continuing this journey with me. What I have learned about the brain from my own personal study, from great researchers and writers in this field, and from working with both struggling and inspiring leaders for more than 20 years is that the principles taught in this book matter. Their presence shapes cultures that produce awesome, positive unforgettables. The absence of these principles shapes cultures that produce painful, negative unforgettables. Simply put, the cultures we create impact our brain, which, in turn, shape the results we experience in leadership, learning, and life.

I wanted to be a college English teacher—that is, until I became a college English teacher. I'm not sure when the realization hit me that this career was not the best fit for me. I'm relatively certain it was late one night in the midst of grading literally hundreds of five-paragraph essays with ridiculous titles.

Don't get me wrong: I love English, and I love English teachers. I'm forever indebted to my many wonderful English professors. It was just that the repetitive nature of my work had trapped my soul. Then came the power of serendipity.

In my brief career funk, a colleague of mine, the brilliant Dr. Sherry Nabors, offered me a job in a pilot program she was helping create and launch at a major communications company. It was a new concept at the time—basic workplace education. Translated, that means an education program at a business where employees have access to basic reading, writing, and math courses. Though I thought the mission was noble, in all honesty I took the offer because it offered more money and an escape from grading those essays.

I hadn't been on the job more than a few months when an employee, age 50-something with more than 25 years on the job, walked into my cubicle. In tears, she shared a painful story of her struggles with learning and her inability to read. In a workplace with rapidly growing demands and complexities, she was terrified of losing her job. Hello, serendipity.

Tapping into empathy and compassion, I watched her cry, held her hand, listened to her, and then responded as any wise teacher would. I paused, cleared my throat, and stated, "I honestly have no idea how to help you."

Seriously? That's all I had to offer? I had been "teaching," or so I thought. I mean, most of my students stayed awake in class and showed some level of improvement. Yes, I received excellent evaluations and feedback, and students even occasionally requested my classes. However, in the face of this beautiful manufacturing worker, with scars on both wrists from carpal tunnel surgery from years of assembling work, I faced something much different. The stakes were higher. I could not fail her. And I could not let her fail herself.

In a short time, our partnership of learning grew into a small group of learners, which evolved into a larger group, which split into two groups, and so on. The stakes grew even higher. These were "left behind" learners with renewed expectations and hopes. My spirit was renewed as well. I wanted to reach over, grab one of them by the neck, unscrew the "lid" and find out what was going on in there!

Why was learning so hard for them? Why weren't my tried-and-true methods of teaching working? Why were we not getting unforgettable results?

I soon realized I was making things too hard.

From there, I developed an all-consuming, burning desire to find the answer to one question: "How does the brain learn?"

My life-changing experience and that life-changing question both surfaced in the early 1990s. Little did I know that at that time I was on a perfectly positioned path: 1990-2000 would eventually be declared the "Decade of the Brain" by U.S. President George H. W. Bush.

As I began seeking answers, searching for solutions, changing majors, annoying professors with unrelenting questions, and conducting my own personal research, an explosion of information on the brain and how it learns became available. These revelations were due in large part to new imaging technologies that allowed scientists to observe the brain while its owner was still alive. Additionally, we had new pathways of communication to get this information out to practitioners in almost-real time. The findings in neuroscience quickly moved beyond the boundaries of medicine, and fields from marketing and architecture to economics and education were eager to apply them as quickly as possible (and maybe a little too eagerly).

Basically, I had a front-row seat to game-changing discoveries and to a rapidly developing field many called "brain-based" learning. As I applied these principles to my workplace education practice and later to leadership programs, I quickly realized that the power of these concepts extended far beyond any classroom. Above all, I learned that applying the basics of brain learning theory naturally brought better results with less effort.

This information was practical. It provided the foundation of "why" and gave greater insight into the "how." I realized that understanding this amazing piece of equipment, which powers thought, decisions, creativity, behavior, innovation, compassion, and empathy, changes the game.

So who needs this information, anyway? My first response is: anyone who needs an environment where the brain can most likely achieve its best. For starters:

- Managers need to know how the brain learns when presenting news about organizational change.
- Supervisors need to know how the brain learns when completing a performance review or motivating an unengaged employee.
- Executives need to know how the brain learns as they prioritize, create mission and value statements, and communicate with shareholders.

- Physicians and healthcare professionals need to know how the brain learns as they deliver information and collaborate under stressful circumstances and strive for quality outcomes.
- National leaders need to know how the brain learns as they establish policy and exercise diplomacy.
- Sports coaches need to know how the brain learns as they develop athletes and communicate with parents and sponsors.
- Teachers need to know how the brain learns to accelerate educational opportunities and create engaging classrooms.
- Parents, for obvious reasons, need to know how the brain learns so they can establish the foundation where greatness begins.

Perhaps, however, a better response to, "Who needs this information?" is: anyone who considers himself or herself a leader, striving for unforgettable results in leading, learning, and life.

Let the revolution begin.

Don't make it hard.

Challenge

| decreasing threat and increasing trust

Threat kills, steals, and destroys. With every decision, we choose to create a culture of challenge or a culture of threat.

Fatima sits in her office with the door closed, breathing deeply and praying for just 15 minutes of peace—no interruptions, demands, problems, or, most of all, complaints. She closes her computer and puts her head in her hands. With heart racing and jaw clenched, she feels the stress crawling up her back and into her shoulders. She questions past decisions, wonders how she got here, and has little hope that things will ever change. She would rather be under a blanket in a dark room than face yet another meeting with no clear direction or purpose.

Challenge

Fatima is a VP in an industry struggling to keep up in a demanding, competitive economy. While her budget and staff have decreased for the last several years, the demands and expectations on her and her team have exponentially increased. She lacks the support she needs to get the job done but isn't exactly clear on what success would look like even if she had adequate time and resources. She feels like she is drowning in unmet expectations and unrealistic demands.

A workplace once known for innovation and sense of community is now a place where people pass each other by in the halls, distracted and disengaged. Departments are suspicious of one another, competing for recognition and a greater slice of the budget. More conversations are spent around "what *could* happen" than around "what *is* happening." Meetings are endless and pointless. Promotion is based on favoritism over merit.

Then there is the impact of Fatima's career on her personal life. While she longs for a home filled with contentment and peace, she lives in one brimming with pressure and demands. She and her husband work long hours to provide for their four children, all in or entering their teenage years.

The spoken and unspoken demands of their "wannabe" affluent community—private schools, club sports, luxury cars—consume their time and divert their income from important investments, such as saving for college. If she's honest, the last time Fatima and her husband had any real personal connection was years ago. Both of them are lost in the abyss of "appearance," "doing," and "stuff."

Overview

An environment of threat is toxic to ideas, results, performance, personal health, relationships, and potential. Why? Because threat impairs and debilitates the brain. In fact, Dr. John Medina in his book, *Brain Rules*, compares threat to arthritis. He makes the powerful point that just as arthritis cripples the body, threat cripples the brain.

If we seek to create highly performing environments where results come naturally and people thrive and become their best, we absolutely *must* minimize threat. If we are seeking meaningful, sustainable results, there is no return in creating an environment characterized by fear, threat, and stress.

In a high-threat environment:

- Negative behavior patterns continue to occur, grow, and infect others. They are ignored and are never directly addressed or reprimanded.
- Team members may play "nice," but there is not a genuine, transparent sharing of thoughts, concerns, and ideas.
- More discussion happens *after* the meeting than *in* the meeting.
- Morale is low due to a feeling of defeat, helplessness, and apathy.

- Real talent sees the job as a launching pad and always has an external focus on the next step rather than how they can contribute where they are.
- Goals and objectives are time-consuming, obligatory exercises that are carried out with little passion and few meaningful results.
- Work is drudgery, and life is not fun.

In contrast, a challenge environment is empowering. A challenge culture recognizes and purposefully minimizes threats to create a safe environment for learning, being, creating, communicating, and growing. It's a culture where all involved make a concerted, continual effort to increase trust and decrease debilitating threat.

In a challenge culture:

- Team members are empowered, excited, and proud to be a part of the team.
- All can bring their best self, and their best brain, to the task.
- Morale and engagement are high, resulting in the free flow of ideas and collaboration.
- Tough problems and tough conversations are faced head-on, courageously and fearlessly, and handled with clarity and consideration.
- Goals and objectives are guides that lead to real, impactful results.
- High performance, innovation, enthusiasm, and fun are the norm rather than the exception.

- People are genuinely welcomed and valued, and have a sense of motivation and belonging.
- Work is fulfilling, and life has purpose.

What makes the difference between a threat environment and a challenge environment? A threat environment "just happens," with leaders and influencers giving no thought and no course correction to a culture that is antagonistic to improving relationships, addressing problems, and aligning to how the brain learns best. A challenge environment happens "on purpose," with leaders and influencers making deliberate decisions to continuously improve relationships, tackle tough problems head-on, and align to how the brain works best.

Reflection

- Describe a time in your life when you were under "threat." (This is a time which, for you, caused undue anxiety, stress, and dread.)
  - What was the personal impact?
  - What changed for you when the threat was no longer present?
- Describe three to five conditions under which you feel "challenge." These are conditions which, for you, give a positive charge, boost energy, and release creativity and excitement. (Ex: Working with a great team, planning a new project, or receiving recognition.)
  - What was the personal impact?

- Think of leaders in your personal experience. Discuss how they impacted the environment (culture).
    - Have you ever left a job because of a leader? What were the circumstances?
    - Have you ever stayed at a job because of a leader? What were the circumstances?

Neurology & Science

The secret to why threat debilitates, and why it is virtually impossible to perform at our best when we are under threat, lies in understanding how threat impacts the brain.

Your brain is a treasure; everyone needs to know this. But understanding a few key discoveries about how the brain learns and processes information and events is transformational. After all, it's the brain (not some technology with a power cord) that fuels us to be our best selves and live our best lives.

For a better understanding of how threat impacts the brain, let's look at what I call "Big Deals" about the brain. While we have a long way to go in understanding the mysterious equipment we all carry between our ears, there are facts we do know that, when applied, can dramatically change the results in every area of our lives.

The first Big Deal relates to a part of the brain called the prefrontal cortex, or PFC, and is located at the front of the frontal lobe. So, here's **Big Deal #1**: Your prefrontal cortex is priceless. This part of your brain influences those functions absolutely critical to leadership and to living our best lives. Some people have even gone as far as calling it the CEO, "the lobe of leadership," or your "Jiminy Cricket." (That was the name of the character representing Pinocchio's conscience for those who may have been deprived of great literature as a child). Let's take a closer look.

The PFC has direct impact on vital activities such as:

- Creativity
- Innovation
- Problem-solving
- Speech
- Empathy
- Character
- Goal-setting (and the ability to follow through in achieving the goals we set)

Additionally, as the very proactive part of our brain, the PFC allows us to think through the consequences of our actions, or "play the movie forward," as we say in our house.

Increased activity in the prefrontal cortex initiates a flood of good chemicals in our brain, including dopamine, adrenaline, epinephrine, and norepinephrine. These chemicals facilitate mood stabilization and motivation, as well as the ability to learn and assimilate new information.

In recent years, even more astonishing research has linked the PFC with various types of self-control which are needed but not accessible when the brain is under threat.

Motor self-control

One type of self-control linked to the PFC is motor self-control. Think of the childhood game, Simon Says. The rules are not complicated; you can move only when "Simon says." That's the function of a neural mechanism in the PFC. However, we now believe that the same neural mechanism in the PFC that controls motor self-control is also responsible for other types of self-control critical to being our best selves and leading others.

Financial self-control

In addition to motor self-control, this neural mechanism heavily influences financial self-control. If you've ever made an impulse buy, you know exactly what I'm talking about. Ever got purchasing fever? That urge to acquire a new purse, a new house, or the latest technology gadget? Financial self-control is seeing the new car, smelling the new car, and envisioning how sophisticated you will look driving up in the new car...and then remembering you can't *afford* the new car! It's the ability to wake up from your daydream and see yourself committing six years of your hard-earned money to buying a car that will depreciate as much as 30% in the first year and 70% by the fourth.

Emotional self-control

This mechanism in the PFC also regulates emotional self-control. It's the ability to manage your emotions—especially under emotionally-charged situations. If you've ever attended a child's sporting event, or better yet, been a parent attending your child's sporting event, then you fully understand what emotional self-control does and does not look like.

But in addition to regulating emotions, it also oversees the ability to stay motivated and disciplined. Several years ago, my sister and I were inspired by our friends who were running long distances and wearing cool running swag from the races in which they participated.

"What a great idea," we thought, one evening around 9:00 p.m.

We were much less enthusiastic when the alarm went off at 5:30 a.m. for us to go out and train in the rain and cold. Actually getting out of bed and putting on those running shoes was most definitely a form of emotional self-control.

Cognitive self-control

This part of the priceless PFC also applies to the ability to control your thoughts. You are better able to discern rational and irrational thoughts when the PFC is fully engaged. We will dig deeper into the power and deception of thoughts later. For now, remember that your thoughts can lie, and you don't have to believe and accept every thought you have.

As I often say, thoughts are a lot like family members: they are familiar and may make us feel good, but when they visit, we don't have to make their room so comfortable that they never want to leave!

Perspective self-control

As if the previous four types of self-control were not enough to juggle, there is also evidence that this magical mechanism controls our ability to truly see a situation from someone else's perspective. Let that sink in for a moment.

Think about how critical the ability to shift perspectives is, especially in reducing threat and building trust. Imagine how many conflicts could be avoided or resolved if we could genuinely see the other person's position. Envision how communication could improve if we could appreciate the listener's or reader's perspective.

Here's the problem. The PFC is highly susceptible to disease and is extremely fragile and prone to injury. It is also particularly vulnerable to hijackings—especially those triggered by negative stress and threat. And this leads to the second "Big Deal" about the brain which involves the part that is activated by threat, commonly referred to as the brain stem.

Big Deal #2: Threat to the brain is threat to the brain. If compared to a city, the PFC is like the brain's city council while the brain stem area is more like the city's gangs. The PFC is proactive and stimulates good chemicals. The brain stem is reactive and stimulates bad chemicals, such as cortisol, that impair sleep, performance, learning, memory, and health. While the PFC prepares for threat, the brain stem responds to threat. Any threat. All threat. Regardless of whether it is physical, like a poisonous snake, or psychological, like a poisonous boss, coworker, or spouse.

Increased activity in the PFC allows us to easily access all of these sophisticated abilities we want for ourselves, those we influence, and those we lead. By increasing activity in the PFC, we stimulate good chemical balance, allowing us to focus, learn, and perform at optimal levels. We "turn on" the priceless functions of things such as speech, willpower, creativity, empathy, and planning.

On the other hand, decreased activity in the PFC deprives us of these sophisticated abilities we want for ourselves, those we influence, and those we lead. By decreasing activity in the PFC, we stimulate bad chemical balance, causing us to react rather than respond, lose sleep, and get sick.

So, the science in brain research gives us a powerful, important warning: when threat enters the scene, all of the priceless functions of the PFC go offline. For all practical purposes, access to all capabilities of the PFC is no longer available when threat appears.

Why, then, would we introduce and allow threat to thrive when the results we are striving for are the domain of the prefrontal cortex?

Application

Recall a few moments from your life:
- When was the last time you were in a large group and unexpectedly called upon to answer a complicated question or report on a project? How articulate were you? Chances are you scrambled

for your thoughts or had the infamous "deer in the headlights" look for an awkward period of time.

- **When was the last time you were reeling in anger? How adept were you at truly seeing the situation from the other person's perspective?** There is a reason why we have the "I am 100% right" syndrome when we are angry. It's because we can't see the issue from any perspective other than our own. The last time you were angry, most likely you were convinced you were 100% right. Then, as time ticked on, the anger calmed, and the PFC came back online, you probably realized you weren't 100% right. And as more time passed, your percentage of being right likely drastically reduced because you had the ability to "put yourself in the other person's shoes."

- **When was the last time you were creative, innovative, energized, lost in the moment, or "in the zone?"** That's a condition Mihaly Csikszentmihalyi named being "in flow." Chances are you were engaged in doing something you loved in an environment conducive to how you operate best. The reason for this joyful, heaven-on-earth, best-self moment is because there was a decrease in threat and an increase in challenge.

If we want an outcome or result that involves being our best self, bringing out the best in others, expressing creativity and innovation, performing to our fullest potential, intelligent communication, and understanding the perspectives of others, then we must seek ways to reduce threat and increase challenge in the environment. Doesn't that sound like the kind of results we want in our workplaces, teams, schools, homes, and relationships?

Let's contrast a threat culture with a challenge culture to see the differences each presents in terms of measurable results. (If you've ever felt like you were working in a dysfunctional environment, where you actually used words like "unhealthy" and "toxic" to describe the culture, feel free to go ahead and insert your own story here!)

STORY #1

Early in my career, after teaching at a university, I landed my first "corporate" job developing a workplace education program for a major communications company. Though I couldn't hear the voice at the time, the culture was laden with threat—it was screaming "dysfunction." Me against you. You against me. Us against them.

The union would not, under any conditions, agree with management. Management would not, under any conditions, agree with the union. Employees were not permitted to attend professional development classes on company time. I once asked for paper clips; I was given two. To explain: Supervisor Jim emailed me to ask if we needed any supplies in the learning center, and I replied with a short list. The most pressing item? Paper clips. He stopped by that afternoon and placed two on my desk.

Challenge

Sounds like a light-hearted practical joke, right? Not at all. He was completely serious.

A more pronounced example of this threat culture happened several months later and involved cheesecake with a side of posturing and humiliation. Our team and Supervisor Jim were invited to a national conference in Miami, Florida. Andy, the head guy in our organization and Jim's boss, attended as well.

Andy told Jim to take the team for a celebration dinner on the eve of the conference banquet. He encouraged Jim to, "Go big!" because "The sky is the limit!" Andy also told Jim to personally cover the meal and the company would reimburse him. So, we went big and racked up an impressive bill. As instructed, Jim personally covered the tab, which was considerably high for a middle manager and sole income provider for his large family.

The next evening, our team, Jim, and Andy gathered around the table at the conference banquet. We enjoyed a wonderful dinner, after which cheesecake was offered as dessert. And it looked delicious! In fact, it was so enticing that Supervisor Jim asked for two pieces when the waiter served our table.

After Jim finished his first piece, he decided he was no longer hungry and offered his second piece to others at the table. There were no takers as everyone was stuffed and content.

All was peaceful until Andy spoke up: "Jim, you WILL eat that cheesecake."

Our initial genuine laughter choked down to a nervous one then quickly dwindled to a "ha...ha...ho...ho..." chuckle with long pauses in between.

Then silence fell.

Andy stood up, stared down at Jim, and said, "You WILL eat every bite of that cheesecake, or I will not approve reimbursement for last night's dinner."

Our team sat in complete silence as we watched our boss unwillingly eat every bite of that second piece. Our heads dropped liked whipped dogs and we empathized with our boss, who had been reduced to a 6-year-old not allowed to leave the table until every pea on his plate was eaten. Embarrassed. Belittled. Humiliated.

It may seem odd, but I consider this experience a privilege, because I can definitely hear the voice in my head yelling loud and clear today: "Dysfunctional! Unhealthy! Toxic!"

From lack of supplies to management styles, this was a culture of threat. Leaders became bigger by making other people feel small. The scarcity mentality (there is not a big enough pie for everyone to have a piece—pardon the pun) ruled. People were driven by fear.

Talent and high performers—such as myself—left as quickly as they could find another opportunity. All were afraid of attempting anything involving risk or demonstrating initiative for fear of failure and reprimand. Few spoke their truth aloud, but most, privately, shared their frustrations and resentments for hours on end.

Meetings were a waste of time, productivity suffered, and the company was not positioned to meet the rapidly changing demands of the communication field.

Today, the parking lot is empty and weeds grow up through the cracks of the concrete. If I were to tell you the name of the company, most of you would go back in the archives in your mind and say, "Yeah, I remember them."

STORY #2

In contrast, my next adventure led me to a defense manufacturing organization. Here, employees attended personal and professional development classes on company time. They were encouraged to attend sessions that were not directly tied to their current positions. If employees aspired to move into a leadership role, they were welcome to take leadership classes.

Novel idea.

I hate to date myself, but the internet as we know it today had only recently become available when I took this job. While other companies had restrictive policies concerning usage and were suspicious of the personal use of this new tool, this company's policy encouraged exploring, learning, and using it.

They knew it was the future, and the greater the skills employees at all levels had with this new amazing technology, the greater the likelihood they would use it to become more efficient, innovative, and productive in their positions.

It was a culture that encouraged collaboration, celebrated accomplishments (large and small), and recognized individuals and teams for outstanding contributions. Managers coached and served rather than bossed. They were promoted based on results and the growth and performance of their teams. Ideas were exchanged, tough issues were placed front and center to address, and every performer had equal opportunity to grow and develop professionally.

In this culture of challenge, leaders became greater by developing other leaders. The abundance mentality prevailed, and the organization operated with the fundamental belief that the pie was big enough for everyone to have a piece (again, no pun intended). It was collaboration over competition.

People were encouraged and rewarded for growing, taking risks, being innovative, and showing initiative. They felt safe to express their ideas and opinions. Talent flocked to interviews, and high performers stayed. Productivity was high, and innovation met the rising challenges. This company is thriving all these years later, surviving mergers, technology changes, and economic ebb and flow.

A culture of challenge is one of trust. A culture of threat is one of distrust. A culture of challenge takes intentional and purposeful action to eliminate debilitating threat and adopt actions that create a safe environment for learning, experimenting, being creative, communicating, developing, and growing.

Top 10 threats that kill results

Challenge is the opposite of threat. Challenge turns on the PFC, while threat shuts it down. Think about the last time you were under physical threat: Maybe a person in a dark parking lot made you feel uncomfortable. Maybe a snake slithered across your foot. Maybe the airplane dropped unexpectedly because of turbulence. Maybe you heard your child scream. I'm guessing you didn't pause and consciously evaluate whether the threat was physical, emotional, or psychological so that you could respond accordingly. Most likely, your heart rate increased, your jaw clenched, you responded with a knee-jerk reaction, and you may have used descriptive language.

Just guessing.

A few years ago, I traveled to Boston to facilitate a workshop. (I'm from Texas, which is an important detail for this story.) It was the middle of winter in Boston, which looks very different from the middle of winter in Texas. Around 3 a.m., the fire alarm went off in my hotel. I came out of a dead sleep and reacted the way any sane person from Texas would—I ran outside into three feet of snow. No coat. No shoes.

Needless to say, the wait for the fire truck was not only miserable but also a little embarrassing. Though there were several of us standing out in the cold, unprepared, others had the forethought to put on shoes and wrap up in a coat; a few overachievers even grabbed hats and gloves.

We'll come back to that story later. For now, it demonstrates some important points. First, my brain, like any brain, simply reacted to threat. In that instance, as in so many others, I never paused to reflect on what kind of threat I was facing. I reacted. In the same way, I don't pause to reflect on the kind of threat I am facing when a ball is flying at my head, a car swerves into my lane, or someone humiliates me in public.

My brain reacts. So does yours. In our reacting, we "lose" our full ability to exercise higher-order critical-thinking skills. The brain simply reacts to threat, whether it is physical (like a poisonous snake) or psychological (like a poisonous comment).

So, what are the top threats that impact performance in the workplace? What are the threats that cultures high in threat allow and cultures high in challenge should be on the lookout to prevent and work to minimize? My list of the Top 10 threats lurking in the workplace are those I have observed, consulted and coached on, and developed learning solutions for over the course of more than 20 years.

Threat #1: Social rejection

In 2011, the University of Michigan studied similarities of physical pain and the pain of social rejection using fMRI—functional magnetic resonance imaging scans. As one article described, during the rejection task, participants who had experienced an unwanted romantic breakup within the last six months viewed a photo of their ex-partner and thought about their feelings.

During the physical pain task, a thermal stimulation device, attached to the participant's forearm, either gave a painful but tolerable stimulation or a non-painful, warm stimulation. The result? Not to over-simplify, but the study found "pain" and "hurt" are very closely related. Similar to Big Deal #2, this study established that in the brain, physical pain and the pain of social rejection are virtually identical. Both "hurt" in very similar ways. The study demonstrated an overlap between these two experiences in two brain regions—the secondary somatosensory cortex and the dorsal posterior insula.

Social rejection can exist in any culture where humans are involved—at any age, of any ethnicity or background, with any title or socioeconomic status. From the team member who feels excluded to the child bullied on the playground, relationships and a feeling of being accepted matters.

Threat cultures exclude; challenge cultures include. Challenge cultures know the value of a sense of belonging and seek ways to ensure that happens. Through formal programs like precepting and mentoring and informal exercises such as teambuilding and interaction with leaders, challenge cultures address the importance of feeling connected to others.

Threat #2: Change

Good or bad, change presents an element of threat. A few years ago, my dishwasher died, and I had a new one installed. Good change, right? Energy efficient, quieter, holds larger loads, blah, blah, blah. The design was different from my old one, causing a major interruption to my OCD-like tendencies of stacking the dishes just so.

My new dishwasher caused me to reevaluate, make adjustments, and learn a new system—to slow down a bit before I could speed back up. Such is the nature of change. Whether it is an improved piece of technology, an adjusted swing for a softball player, or a new organizational chart, change causes a hiccup in the flow of life. Your brain strives for homeostasis, the tendency for processes and systems to stay stable and consistent. This is an awesome quality for your blood pressure and body temperature. It can, however, be a major obstacle when it comes to changing thoughts and well-established behaviors.

Threat cultures plow through change with very little consideration for processing time, additional training and support, or giving the compelling reasons for the alterations. They are rarely successful in implementing large-scale changes and blame others or outside forces for the failure. Challenge cultures know that change is easy until it involves humans. Therefore, they evaluate the resources needed for a successful change, allow adequate time and provide support, and follow a calculated, proven change management process.

Threat #3: Unrealistic standards

I've noticed that when people I coach are faced with standards they do not have the resources or capabilities to meet, the result can leave them feeling devastated and hopeless. They begin to use words like "drowning," "overwhelmed," "frustrated," and "discouraged." It's easy to catastrophize these situations because not meeting expectations is threat and hinders the brain from working at peak performance.

Situations where we are caught in the trap of unrealistic standards always reminds me of one of my favorite books, Joseph Heller's classic novel *Catch-22*. Essentially, a Catch-22 represents an unrealistic standard, an unsolvable problem, a lose-lose situation. It is a crazy-maker. It shows up in all areas of life: Professionally, as a demand to produce more without the necessary time and resources. Academically, as a requirement to pass a standardized test without the resources to prepare for the test. Personally, as a desire to please an addicted spouse whose erratic behavior cannot be pleased. Catch-22 situations can pop up in any area of our lives. And when they do, our brain is under threat.

In threat cultures, standards are unrealistic— sometimes they cannot be humanly accomplished, and sometimes they are unclear or elusive, moving targets. In challenge cultures, however, not only are standards clear and measured, they also reflect the values by which the standards are to be accomplished. People have involvement and ownership in establishing such standards, and accomplishments toward achieving them are recognized and rewarded.

Threat #4: Lack of resources

I often say Threat #4 is the best friend of Threat #3 because the two are virtually inseparable. The threat of unrealistic standards is most often felt because of a lack of resources. Threat results when there is a lack of any resource: time, money, health, and people.

The father of brain-based learning, Eric Jensen, is passionate about educating teachers in the differences among children living and learning in impoverished areas. He points out in *Teaching with Poverty in Mind* that the poverty problem is not solely about money, as most people assume. Rather, these children are at a disadvantage because of a number of inadequate resources. They lack stability as they move twice as often and get evicted five times as often as other children. They lack safety as they are six times greater to be in pedestrian accidents as other children. They lack encouragement as significant adults in their lives, such as teachers, do not expect them to achieve as they do for other children. Additionally, they lack health resources, moral support resources, nutritional resources, and on and on.

The cumulative effect of these deficiencies impacts performance of all types—academic, relationship, individual accomplishment, and so forth. A lack of resources can create a vicious cycle of threat culture, underperformance, and hopelessness. With many groups I encounter, expectations are high but resources are unreasonably minimal. Clearly, there is a fine line. We want to streamline and operate as leanly as possible to maximize resources and maintain a competitive edge. Threat happens when the culture is streamlined to the extreme, with employees doing jobs that once were fulfilled by two or three or more people.

Working recently with one of my client organizations, team members were expected to acquire the skills to implement a new piece of medical equipment, but there was a freeze on training and professional development.

Budgets are always tight, and this trend is likely to continue. It's not all bad, because it forces organizations to run lean, be innovative, and exercise good stewardship. We do have technology that, in theory, should allow us to do more, more efficiently, with fewer assets. In reality, however, the workload increases at lightning speed while the people, financial, and time resources plummet. Unlike threat cultures, challenge cultures assess and address the resources necessary to meet the expectations.

Threat #5: Risk of loss

Clearly, loss represents threat. And it can appear in innumerable ways. One that is common in organizations is job loss. But while job loss may initially seem an obvious threat, a job represents much more than a literal place where a person is employed, receives a paycheck and health benefits, and participates in a 401K plan.

Certainly, losing any of those things is a threat. But a broader context has, sadly, begun to take shape more frequently in our society and daily news cycle, and I faced it on the very day I wrote this chapter: I attended a friend's funeral. She had been shot by an employee whom she was terminating. He killed her, then killed himself. It was such a sad, needless ending that should elevate awareness of mental illness and the seriousness of acknowledging the impact of threat.

A person's job can be his identity, her safety net and means of security, her place in life, or his position in life. After all, one of the most commonly asked questions after small talk about the weather with a new acquaintance is, "What do you do for a living?" For better or worse, in so many ways our jobs define how others see us and how we see ourselves.

There are many life events that carry the same losses we suffer when a job ends. Divorce, death, health issues, relocation, the empty nest, and retirement often involve the loss of identity and security. And all these life situations impact our workforce each day they enter the building. In challenge cultures, risk of loss is certainly a threat that leaders are mindful of, not only for the impact it can have personally but also for the impact it has on those they seek to lead and influence.

Threat #6: Humiliation

Humiliation is the act of degrading, disgracing, and shaming. It is a threat that is too often very real in our workplaces, schools, and homes—like Supervisor Jim, humiliated over the cheesecake incident. In another case,

I knew a bright young girl who struggled with tests. She scored below the designated percentage on a standardized test and wasn't allowed to go on the end-of-school field trip with her class. She was humiliated. I also recently encountered a supervisor who, behind closed doors, continuously referred to one of his team members as "that goofy bastard." That's humiliating, and the employee didn't even know it.

In challenge cultures, humiliation, whether public or private, is a non-negotiable. No one should be exposed to such unacceptable behavior; it may be the most severe and crippling of all threats. A challenge culture establishes values and holds people accountable for not only what they do but how they do it.

Threat #7: Micromanaging

On the surface, micromanaging comes across as a lack of trust in others. One client of mine had a boss who asked her to take minutes in meetings but would rewrite her minutes before distributing them to the team.

When we micromanage, it can appear that we do not have confidence in the ability or ethics of those who work with and for us. In reality, however, micromanaging really occurs because we do not have confidence and trust in ourselves.

That may sound odd. And it should. People tend to micromanage when they are trying to control. And people try to control when they feel insecure. On the one hand, we believe that micromanagers have overwhelming confidence in their own ability and believe that they—more than anyone else—possess the ability to make the "right" decision or get the job done "right." On closer reflection, though, our need to control situations and people is always rooted not in confidence but in fear—fear of the unknown, fear of the future, or fear in our ability.

One of my favorite learning scenes comes from one of my favorite movies, "Apollo 13." The engineers realize the astronauts are slowly being poisoned by carbon monoxide gas. The lead engineer upends a box of random items the astronauts have at their disposal onto a table and gives very simple instructions to the team. It's a literal square-peg-through-a-round-hole problem.

The engineering team dives right in, no micromanagement necessary. NASA's upper management wasn't concerned with charts, graphs, or reports. In today's terms, they never asked to see an Excel spreadsheet or a PowerPoint presentation. The Apollo 13 engineers simply had a clear direction and knew their available resources. Upper management delegated full authority to get the job done. And they did.

A threat culture is one where leadership is suspect of others' capabilities, delegates small tasks rather than authority, and is fueled by ego. In a challenge culture, leadership trusts they have hired capable professionals, gives them the freedom and authority to be capable professionals, and supports rather than controls the team.

Threat #8: Lack of trust

In *Speed of Trust: The One Thing that Changes Everything*, author Stephen M.R. Covey explains trust as that space where character overlaps competence. If either is missing, or if both do not exist consistently over time, there is not trust.

Consider this scenario: you have an upcoming surgery—it's rare, risky, and potentially fatal if all does not go as planned. There are only two doctors on the planet available to be your surgeon. You have to choose.

Do you go with Doctor #1? She created the procedure and is world-renowned for her attention to detail. However, she is arrogant, rude, and unwilling to listen to you, your family, or the hospital staff. Though she has performed hundreds of successful surgeries, her unwillingness to listen to others' input has resulted in past surgery complications and fatalities.

Or do you go with Doctor #2? He didn't pioneer the surgery but has a successful track record. He listens to your concerns fully, explains details in a way you can understand, and receives high marks for bedside manner. He has compassion for his patients and their family, and is an excellent communicator with hospital staff.

I'm willing to bet that most of us would be inclined to choose Doctor #2. Why? While Doctor #1 has demonstrated competence, Doctor #2 has demonstrated competence and character. Most often we have choices in physicians, so in some ways that's an unfair example. But rarely do we have a choice with teachers, government leaders, or bosses (and definitely not with our parents). In those cases, we "get what we get." Hopefully, these people have both character and competence. When they are missing one, trust is low and threat is high.

These two traits are important ingredients in trust. As Covey suggests, leadership success is the result of character and competence in balance. Leadership failure is always the result of imbalanced character and competence; one or the other is lacking. The third ingredient I would add, a third "C" in this trust equation, is consistency. Trust is character and competence, lived out consistently over time. Consistency is key. As we've all experienced, trust can take a lifetime to build and a millisecond to destroy.

Threat cultures are low-trust cultures, and low trust in a culture carries serious costs. Author Francis Fukuyama compares low trust to an unnecessary tax, a powerful metaphor. High trust societies get to avoid the tax; low trust societies must pay the tax.

The question is, "What tax, or unnecessary costs are you paying because of low trust?" Low trust is like second-hand smoke, a toxic poison in the culture. Low trust produces blaming, finger pointing, criticizing, condemning, complaining, and dissension. Professionally or personally, we have all witnessed the consequences of low trust and the devastating tax that naturally results.

Challenge cultures simply do not have to pay the tax that threat cultures do. Relationships in challenge cultures do not suffer the consequences that relationships in threat cultures do. Threat kills, steals, and destroys. Trust yields life, speed, and quality.

Threat #9: Favoritism

My daughter plays softball in select or "club" organizations. Where we live, fastpitch softball is wildly popular, competitive, and, at times, cut-throat. I've jokingly said throughout the years that I sold my soul to the softball gods; how easily it became overly competitive and all-consuming for me. Nevertheless, I pack the cooler, load the car, and spend most weekends sitting behind the cage in a folding chair with the rest of the crazy Softball Moms.

I've learned there is only one thing more insane and unpredictable than a Softball Mom—a Softball Dad. Because their daughters have the ability to play ball, these dads believe they have the ability to coach. And coach they do. We moms fondly call this phenomenon "Daddy Ball."

When tryouts roll around and teams post that "all positions are open," they are telling a partial truth. What they really mean is that all positions are open, except for the positions reserved for the daughters of Daddy Coach #1, Daddy Coach #2, and Daddy Coach #3. Such favoritism will diminish the enthusiasm of the other players, hinder the coaches from being objective and effective, and ultimately hold the team back from performing at its best.

This example is similar to what we see in a workplace with a threat culture. Favoritism shows up in multiple forms, such as to whom projects are assigned (or not assigned), to whom special privileges like telecommuting are afforded (or not), rewards and recognition given (or withheld), and so forth.

The impact on a workforce parallels that of the softball world. The enthusiasm of other team members diminishes, the leader's objectivity and effectiveness is hindered, and the team, as well as the company, will never achieve its best. The other high-performing "players" will seek to "play" for another team.

Threat #10: Lack of meaning

As a consultant, I work with companies interested in keeping talented employees and keeping them engaged. Not surprisingly, the most frequently cited reason for leaving a position is due to leadership. Have you ever left a job because of your leader? I have.

What is the most frequently cited reason for staying? What is the most frequently cited driver of engagement? Oftentimes, the most frequent answer falls under the heading of "meaningful purpose." This is especially true for millennials. People want to feel like they are making progress and are contributing to something greater than themselves.

We will delve more deeply into this topic in the next chapter, but for now, let's just say that meaning matters. It matters at all ages and in all situations. In threat cultures, people work for a paycheck. In challenge cultures, people work for a purpose. Attention is given to communicating the impact of great work on the team, on the organization, in the community, and in the world. Because purpose is as important as pay, team members in challenge cultures have a greater sense of mission and commitment to the vision.

Threat culture vs. challenge culture

A challenge culture results when threats are recognized, addressed, and minimized on purpose. This creates a safe environment where people can be their best self.

Rather than social rejection and exclusivity, challenge cultures actively promote acceptance and inclusion. People have a voice, feel valued and appreciated, and have a sense of belonging. All are welcome to bring their whole self, including their differences, to every situation.

Rather than ignoring the impact of change, challenge cultures acknowledge change and seek ways to turn it into exciting opportunities. Resistance is anticipated, expected, and processed in a healthy way, with transition time, along with appropriate training, resources, and tools provided to ensure the change is successful. Wins of all sizes are acknowledged and celebrated.

Rather than unrealistic and unclear standards, challenge cultures clearly and continuously communicate expectations, as well as live out and model them. Training, resources, and tools are in place to reach these expectations. Progress is measured, recognized, and rewarded.

Rather than insufficient resources, challenge cultures provide the right resources at the right time. Team members are set up to succeed and are encouraged to use their creativity and innovation without fear of failing.

Rather than fear of job and identity loss, challenge cultures are marked by direct and open communication. Instead of allowing stories to evolve in a cloud of mystery, communication is transparent—even when the message is unpopular. In addition, leaders in this type of environment think strategically, continuously focusing on helping others identify strengths, look ahead, set goals, take initiative, and create clear road maps for achievement.

Rather than using humiliation as a form of control, challenge cultures use feedback and engagement as motivation. Leaders spend less time focusing on what someone is doing wrong, more time on what they are doing right, and how they can better leverage individual strengths to improve in all areas.

Rather than micromanaging, challenge cultures honor input and seek ways for people to have a choice and a voice. Leaders in this culture are coachable and always willing to learn. There is no "my way or the highway" at work; rather, it's an effort to co-create "our way." Leaders invest in building their team and empower team members to make decisions. They delegate authority, not just tasks.

Rather than a lack of trust, challenge cultures are characterized by consistency. Leaders in these environments are dependable, predictable (within reason), and consistent. Their employees, clients, and peers can rely on them to be transparent; they openly admit mistakes and are willing to correct and redirect based on what's best for the team rather than what's best for their ego. People who work, learn, or live with leaders in challenge cultures know that, without a doubt, their leader "has their back" and their best interest in mind, all day and every day, and feel encouraged to voice their opinions and share their ideas.

Rather than favoritism, challenge cultures give a fair chance to anyone willing to make the investment, aspire to a new level of performance, and get the work done. There is no "Daddy Ball" in a challenge culture. The rewards are based on performance, progress, and heart.

Rather than lack of meaning, challenge cultures are vision-driven. Everyone knows the greater impact and purpose, and how daily tasks—even seemingly mundane ones—align with the vision to achieve a worthwhile outcome. They care as much about purpose as pay.

Final notes about threat

Before you leave this chapter, here are two final important points. First, threat is all about perception. What is threat to one brain may not be to another.

Let's return to my experience with the hotel fire alarm in Boston. In that situation, my brain perceived the alarm as threat, and I simply reacted. Others experiencing the exact same set of circumstances may not have interpreted the situation as threat.

Imagine a seasoned business traveler in the room next to mine. He may have laid out his coat, shoes, hat, and gloves prior to going to bed—just in case of an emergency. He may have studied the emergency exit map and strategy on the back of the hotel door. He may have been awake at 3 a.m., finishing the greatest novel he had ever read. He may have been waiting his whole life to be present for a hotel fire, preparing to rescue frightened people. When the alarm sounded and the light flashed, he may have recognized the situation not as a threat but as an opportunity. If so, his reaction would have been quite different than mine. Instead of scurrying thoughtlessly around, he may have gotten out of bed with an enthusiastic energy, calmly dressed, and walked out of the building looking for people to help along the way.

Clearly, the same set of circumstances can present themselves differently to different people. What is threat to one brain may not be to another. In Boston, as it turns out, there never was a threat; the smoke detector in one room had simply malfunctioned.

The brain reacts whether or not the threat is real or perceived. If someone sees favoritism or lack of honesty in an environment, the brain reacts to threat. True or imagined, when the brain processes threat, performance is impacted.

My second point about threat is, not all threat is bad. Fear can protect us. If we see a wild animal running loose or a menacing person lurking in the shadows, we course-correct. Fear can motivate us. Ever worked extra hard on a presentation because you were afraid of looking incompetent in front of your leadership and peers? (I have.) Or, ever hustled to meet a deadline because you thought you might lose your job or a client? (I definitely have.) The presence of healthy fear can absolutely be a good thing.

"Bad" threat, the kind of threat we've been talking about in this chapter that results in increased problems and decreased results, has certain characteristics. Dr. Medina describes such threat in "Brain Rules" as a stressor that is perceived as negative and arouses a physiological response. We can literally feel the triggers going off in our body. Negative stress is perceived by the person as aversive, as my experience in the Boston hotel proved. And finally, negative stress occurs when the person experiencing the threat does not feel in control of the stressor.

A friend of mine is an executive at a company that makes concrete, where physical safety is paramount. In fact, when entering the building, a red light/green light scoreboard updates everyone on physical injuries in the workplace. Next to the light is a sign that reads, "Number of days without accident." When they reach a certain number of accident-free days, they have a celebration, and team members are rewarded. Such a practice is common. Clearly, we want workplaces that are safe—physically.

But what about emotional and psychological safety? Are those days tracked as well? After all, threat to the brain is threat to the brain—regardless if the threat is physical or psychological. This is a sobering point that carries a very special, personal meaning to me, the funeral of the friend I mentioned earlier when discussing risk of loss. She was a supervisor in a high-threat culture. She brought an employee into her office to fire him. He fired her—with five gunshots that took her away from a husband who loved her dearly, four children who needed her desperately, and a world of contribution left unfulfilled. Threat cultures are toxic. They carry costs. They cause damage—sometimes irreparable, eternal damage.

Relevance

| leading with vision and strengths

Imagine a culture in complete alignment...each individual using his or her strengths to drive a united purpose.

I t's a cold Wednesday morning, and daylight is just beginning to appear as Greg drives through the gates and to the front section of the parking lot. He finishes the last drops of his coffee, grabs his lunch, locks the door, and reaches for his badge. This is a familiar routine, one he has performed for nearly 26 years at a defense manufacturing facility.

He says, "Hello," to the guard at the gate and jokes for a minute about the game last night, flashes his badge, and walks through the turnstile. Employees are slowly filtering into the building, much like zombies, not quite awake during these early-morning hours. Greg passes through the break room for a second cup of coffee to jump-start his day and exchanges casual, "Good mornings," with a few co-workers he's known for years.

His boss passes by, stops, and sticks his head into the break room. He says, "Hey Greg, remember the training team is planning on doing some observations this morning. Are you OK with answering some of their questions and showing them around?"

"No problem," Greg replies. After all, he has the longest tenure in the quality department and looks forward to a break in the dull routine of the day.

He heads toward his workstation, where he glances at the pictures of his family. They are his pride and joy, his reason for getting up so early every morning and going to a job that is, on most days, unfulfilling. The pictures are secured by a magnet on a small whiteboard, which also includes a daily countdown. Greg plans to work 1,195 more days before retiring. For motivation, he started this countdown, which he edits every morning. He checks his personal email quickly before the tasks on the assembly line begin.

Greg has been learning after-hours to create websites for a few small companies in his community. In the last year, he has discovered a real talent for creating impactful websites and loves that he gets lost and fully engaged when he's creating them. When he retires, he plans on doing web design full-time.

Later in the morning, Greg is working in his role as the last stop for quality inspection when the training team shows up. They are creating training modules for new hires, and part of the process is conducting a job-task analysis with experienced employees like Greg. They ask several questions about the process he follows, seeking short cuts, tips, suggestions, and so forth. Then they ask where the part Greg is inspecting ultimately goes when it leaves him.

Greg thinks for a minute, points to the next station, and says, "It goes to packing."

Then Greg walks to the break room for a final cup of coffee.

Overview

Relevance is about inspiring and motivating—motivating the workforce through an environment of meaningful, life-giving purpose, both individually and collectively. A relevant environment is one where the workforce is motivated because of two intentional leadership choices.

The first is the choice to motivate by leading with vision, values, and purpose, and to communicate these things in such a way that everyone in the organization owns it. The second is to motivate by leading with strengths and leveraging these strengths to make sure the right people are in the right positions so they do what they love and what they are designed to do.

In cultures that disregard Relevance:

- There is no compelling, guiding vision.
- The values of the organization are unclear, and people are not held accountable to adhere to them.
- Teams work in silos with little understanding of how their work impacts other teams.
- The "how" and the "what" is communicated more than the "why."
- People do not feel a sense of meaning or purpose in what they are doing.
- The workforce is not privy to the bigger picture behind requests, processes, or change.
- More attention is given to deficits and closing performance gaps than to identifying and building strengths.
- The workforce is not invited to bring all their gifts and talents to work.
- Motivation is low because of the lack of clarity and overall purpose.

In contrast, a relevant culture is highly motivating. Leadership intentionally involves others in creating a compelling vision and continuously communicates that vision to bring unity and focus. In addition, leadership knows the power of building on and purposefully seeks to identify each individual's strengths, passions, and aspirations to create development plans that do more than close gaps. Rather, they inspire and allow individuals to reach their full potential.

In a Relevant culture:

- All are involved in creating a vision that is meaningful and inspiring.
- All know how what they do on a daily basis impacts those around them and contributes to the whole.
- All are clear about the forces driving innovation and change.
- The workforce understands the "why" behind the "how" and the "what."
- Leaders have conversations with team members about strengths, talents, and goals, and create customized development plans around what's important to the team member.
- Leaders delegate authority rather than tasks in ways that build on team members' strengths.
- Leaders make smart hiring choices to bring the right strengths to the table.
- The workforce finds meaning and purpose in what they do...every day.

Cultures that embrace relevance shift their focus from competing to collaborating. Individuals and teams do not operate independently, with different visions, values, and goals. Rather, the organization is in complete alignment where each individual uses his or her strengths to drive a united vision and greater purpose. And, relevant cultures shift the focus from deficits to strengths. Individual strengths are assessed, discussed, and leveraged to carry out the mission.

Reflection

- From memory, write out what you know about your organization's:
  - Mission statement
  - Vision statement
  - Guiding values
- In your experience, how well does your organization "walk the talk?"
- In what ways does your work contribute to the mission?
- What percentage of time at work do you spend doing what you do best?
- Describe a time when your leader had a conversation with you about your experience, strengths, and aspirations.
- Would you say your performance reviews are "deficit-focused" (looking at where you fall short and need to improve) or "strengths-focused" (looking at what you do well and how you could do more of that)?

Neurology & Science

In the previous chapter, I shared what I call the Big Deal #1 about the brain. Essentially, it's that our prefrontal cortex (PFC) is priceless, the seat of being our best self. It is the control center for all of those priceless functions we want operating every minute of every day (or at least every work day). It oversees things like planning, taking responsibility, thinking through the consequences of choices and actions, and having thoughtful conversations where we can see situations from various perspectives. Clearly, we are human, and no one can do this every second of every day (or even every work day). But we can activate this part of our brain more if we create a brain-friendly environment. We can leverage more of the PFC for longer time periods when we incorporate the principle of relevance.

Why? I've identified four reasons why the brain performs better and more efficiently when operating in an environment of relevance.

Reason #1: Whole-to-parts

Consider this: I invite you to my house for puzzle night. (Just go with it for a moment.) You walk in and sit down at the kitchen table, and I throw out a 5,000-piece puzzle. Remember, you accepted the invitation. What would your first question most likely be? "Where's the box?"

At least that would display a picture of what this thing is supposed to be when we are finished. This answers the question, "What are we working toward?"

One of the reasons you want to know what the finished puzzle would look like is because that's the way the average brain learns best—whole-to-parts. A picture really is worth a thousand words. Take vision statements, for example. In one study, David Rock, founder of the Neuroleadership Institute, found that when someone is reading a vision statement, the visual cortex in the brain lights up as indicated by MRI. In many ways, vision statements act like the puzzle box picture; they leverage the average brain's desire to learn "whole-to-parts."

When we think "whole-to-parts," we remember to keep the "big picture" as the big picture when it comes to organizational alignment, change initiatives, and important communications.

Reason #2: Neural networks

We spend a lot of time these days building our social networks and encouraging people to reach their career goals by leveraging the relationships in their existing social networks. This same concept holds true when it comes to your brain. It has well-established neural networks, and we learn more efficiently when we leverage these relationships, these existing neural networks.

Let's stand in awe for a moment of neural networks. If you are capable of higher cognitive thought, which you are because you are reading this book, thank your neural networks. Your brain is made up of two kinds of cells: neurons and glial cells. Glial cells make up about 90% of the cells, and though they carry out many important functions, they do not carry nerve impulses. Neurons, on the other hand, exchange signals with each other to form highly complex neural networks.

No one knows exactly how many neurons the typical brain has; estimates range from 50 billion to 500 billion.

Relevance

Let's just say the typical brain has "a lot." Some scientists believe it isn't necessarily the number of brain cells you have (which is really good news for some of us who may not have always made the smartest decisions earlier in life, especially during the college days...); what really counts is the number of connections you have. I once heard one scientist predict the number of possible connections equals the number of leaves on every tree in every forest in the world. Whether this is true, we do know the possible number of connections is numerically mind blowing.

In the simplest terms, neurons are made up of cell bodies, dendrites, and axons. The cell body is the central mass. Dendrites receive information and carry it to the cell body. Axons transmit information and carry it away from the cell body. Terminal buttons, like little parking spaces or key holes, are located at the end of each axon and release neurotransmitters, chemicals that activate neighboring neurons. The junction or gap between the axon of one neuron and the dendrites of a neighboring neuron is called the synapse or synaptic cleft. The presynaptic neuron is the signal-sending cell, and the postsynaptic neuron is the signal-receiving cell.

When the cell body is triggered by an action potential (a change in the electrical potential on the cell's surface), neurotransmitter molecules pour into the synaptic cleft. When the molecules reach the postsynaptic cell, they attach to matching receptor sites. This forms a connection or network with other neurons.

One widely accepted theory about neural networks is the Hebbian Theory, named after renowned neuroscientist Donald Hebb. He proposed that the connection strength among synaptic cells increases as cells are simultaneously activated. Thus, the common saying "cells that fire together, wire together." So, when we experience and learn new things, we build new neural networks and strengthen existing ones.

Think of neural networks as an information transportation system in the brain. Neural networks and their efficiency are sort of like the differences in farm-to-market roads, highways, and interstates.

When we are first introduced to a new concept or task, our brains begin to build a neural network. At this point, that network is similar to a farm-to-market road. You know, those roads most of us end up on when we are completely lost, usually at night, when it's foggy or raining? They are the winding, rocky, narrow roads found far from the interstate. Can you imagine traveling from California to New York on farm-to-market roads? It would be a long, arduous, and frustrating journey; we might even give up.

Such is the case when we are learning something completely brand new or when we are asked to make a change in something that is a well-established behavior or well-worn habit. For example, I play piano. Today, reading music and matching the right notes comes relatively easy. But this was not always the case—just ask my poor parents. My feet didn't touch the floor, my fingers were too small to reach an entire octave, and my brain struggled to read the notes and tell my fingers where to go. I was the child my parents begged to stop practicing. I had a farm-to-market neural network for piano.

Once a neural network is established, however, we can begin to strengthen and build on it. To continue with my analogy, it's like an upgrade from a farm-to-market road to a highway. Though we can definitely go faster and the trip is less frustrating, we are still not hitting top speed and full efficiency. We may have two lanes on the highway, but we all know about construction backups, traffic accidents, and red lights. Those kinds of distractions, interruptions, and setbacks can cause delay.

It's similar in the brain. For me on the piano, I could, in time, match my fingers to the correct notes with relative ease if the music was simple and had lots of repetition. Early on, I could not have performed in front of an audience, but my confidence was growing and my ability was improving. I no longer had to pause as much when a note was a sharp or a flat, and my fingers flowed much more smoothly on the keys. The notes actually began to sound like music, and my parents complained less. My neural network was getting stronger.

Once we have a skill or a subject area mastered, our neural network is similar to a super interstate. The road is firmly established, it is clear of obstacles, and there are multiple lanes of traffic, which allows for greater speed and fewer accidents. We may even hit cruise control from time-to-time. Such is the case now when I play the piano; I no longer have to think about the mechanics of playing and am free to "get lost" in the music.

Warning: Mentally moving from a farm-to-market road to a super interstate doesn't happen overnight. In fact, the process of building a strong neural network can be extremely time-consuming and can vary from individual to individual, depending on aptitude and desire. The brain takes a lot longer to become an expert than most of us think it should. And studies have shown that subject-matter experts are the worst predictors of how long it takes for someone to learn a new skill. For some reason, we tend to forget the struggles it took to learn the skills (such as playing piano) and severely underestimate how long it will take for a newbie to get up to speed.

In one study Sian Beilock talks about in her book, *Choke*, a mobile phone company was attempting to determine how long it would take for consumers to master the new technology. The tech-savvy subject-matter experts estimated it would take the novice 13 minutes to master all of the phone skills. In reality, it took around 30 minutes.

Some studies indicate the brain can require as much as 10,000 hours of intentional practice to master a skill. Of course, that depends on a variety of variables, not least of which is a person's natural aptitude. For example, I'm not sure 10,000 hours of intentional practice would enable me to master my golf game. Rumor has it that Cirque de Soleil® performers may practice a skill up to 30,000 hours before performing it in a show. The point is that they practice a a very long time before they are ready to do it on stage for an audience. And some of us, including me, can't imagine performing the skills in their shows even with 30,000 hours of practice. The gist is this: building a new skill or changing an existing one takes time and can be different for each person.

Eric Jensen cautions that the brain requires much more time to process than originally thought. Of course, it depends on the type of learning. He distinguishes between simple learning and complex learning. "Simple learning" doesn't require a lot of time at all. For example, if I put my hand on a hot stove, I can learn very quickly not to do that again.

"Complex learning" of a complicated task or concept, however, can require an extraordinary amount of time. Of course, there are an endless number of variables that can impact the time the brain takes to learn, including natural ability, interest, capacity, engagement, novelty, interaction, and so forth. The important take-away is that the brain takes time to build an interstate-type of neural network. In fact, Jensen emphasizes that there is no replacement for time.

When we utilize relevance by building on familiar, existing neural networks—such as our strengths, prior experiences, and desires for the future—performance and learning become natural, easier, faster, more meaningful, and more fun.

Reason #3: Lowers threat

In the last chapter, I revealed Big Deal #2: Threat to the brain is threat to the brain. The key point about this big deal is that the brain doesn't pause, and then react differently based on physical threat or emotional threat. And, the brain doesn't really care if the threat is perceived or real. The performance of the brain is most definitely compromised, if not entirely debilitated, by threat.

Relevance helps the brain learn faster and more efficiently because it brings familiarity, which lowers threat. Relevance doesn't focus on all that I can't do, my deficits or my "gaps," which can result in humiliation and failure. Relevance focuses on everything I can do, what I'm naturally good at doing, and what I enjoy, which leverages expertise, comfort, and confidence.

I remember years ago teaching an introductory class on Microsoft Word. How introductory, you ask? Well, let's just say we started by practicing the 'double click.' (No dinosaurs were injured in the telling of this story!) The class was offered to seasoned, savvy administrative assistants who were experts in their jobs; however, they had never used Microsoft Word.

Beyond teaching how to use the software, my job was also to reduce their fear to help them believe they already knew the basics—that this tool was not as foreign as they thought. My task was to build on whole-to-parts, leverage existing neural networks, and reduce threat. Here was my approach: Though the assistants may have never stored files electronically, they had organized files in a designated file cabinet, a drawer, and a folder with a specific name. Though they may have never created an electronic document, they had drafted documents on a typewriter for years and knew the steps necessary for formatting and making corrections. Though they may have never saved a document electronically, they all knew the importance of saving a document. You get the idea.

When we lower threat by making the environment safe and attaching the unknown to the known, our brains become more receptive. Learning is faster. Change is easier. Life is more fun.

Reason #4: Reward system

The brain's reward system is a group of structures in the brain that respond to stimuli the brain finds rewarding, reinforcing, or pleasurable. Like other systems, the brain's reward system is highly complex. But, for our purposes, let's think about it as a stage. The leading actor on the brain stage is the neurotransmitter dopamine. Other supporting actors, all part of the mesolimbic dopamine pathway, include the ventral tegmental area (VTA), the nucleus accumbens, and the frontal lobes.

When the brain's reward system is activated, the VTA releases dopamine, and the mesolimbic dopamine pathway transports it to the nucleus accumbens and the frontal lobes. When dopamine is delivered to the nucleus accumbens, dopamine levels rise, elevating desire, motivation, and reward. When dopamine is delivered to the frontal lobes, also involved in motivation and reward, the brain has a greater capacity to focus and regulate impulsivity.

The reward system raises a couple of important questions. First, what does dopamine do for the brain? Well, it is involved in a number of functions, including attention, focus, memory, mood, sleep, and pleasure. It's often referred to as a "feel good" chemical because it is released and increased during certain kinds of rewarding moments. Clearly, the role of dopamine becomes complicated when triggered by negative stimulus such as illicit drugs. But in the case of learning and leadership, elevated dopamine levels can result in greater attention and focus, stronger motivation, increased productivity, and decreased impulsivity.

Think about the last time you were engaged in doing something you love—like a hobby. I'll wager you were intensely focused, you lost track of time because you were highly engaged and motivated, and you were productive. Part of the magic of that moment was elevated dopamine.

A second question is: What, then, triggers the brain's reward system? In other words, what does the brain consider a reward? There are many reasons why this system is triggered, ranging from chocolate cake to sex. And like in the case of elevated dopamine, these triggers may not always have positive consequences.

One useful model for triggering the brain's reward system in the workplace, created by Dr. David Rock, is called SCARF. The SCARF model includes five domains which are thought to trigger the brain's reward system:

Status: This involves our sense of worth and where we fit into the work hierarchy—both socially and organizationally. Status is about our relative importance to others.

Certainty: This involves having clarity and confidence. Certainty concerns our being able to predict the future.

Autonomy: This involves ownership and control. Autonomy involves a person's sense of control over what they do and the events that occur.

Relatedness: This involves our social relationships. Relatedness is a sense of safety with others—of friend rather than foe.

Fairness: This involves equal opportunity, or a level playing field. Fairness is a perception of even exchanges between people.

Though the SCARF model, and others like it, are useful in examining how to trigger the brain's reward system in general, the reality is that reward and motivation to the brain is personal and specific to the individual. Just as threat to one brain may not be threat to another, reward and pleasure to one brain may not be reward and pleasure to another.

Application

A relevant culture is one that puts these brain-based learning principles into action. Environments that are relevant are those that keep the big picture the big picture.

In addition, environments that are relevant are those that are relentless in discovering and building on strengths. Leaders in relevant environments are both vision-centered and strength-centered.

Vision-centered

Leaders who leverage the power of relevance make sure that strategy, change initiatives, important communications, processes, presentations, and meetings are presented whole-to-parts. Everyone, at every level, understands and owns the larger mission, vision, values, and purpose. And, the entire organization is in big-picture alignment.

Let's look more closely at how relevant environments incorporate the whole-to-parts model of learning. In a sense, whole-to-parts allows us, at all times, to see how all of the parts work together and come together. Whole-to-parts allows us to have a secure, focused sense of direction. Think about going to a shopping mall or to an amusement park: If, at any time, you get lost or confused, you can go to a directory or a park map and look at the layout in its entirety. There you will usually find a red arrow with a "You are here" marker. This allows you to regain your bearings and direction, and you can begin to process the design of the building or layout of the land.

Switching back to a metaphor I used earlier in this chapter, let's focus on assembling a puzzle. Most of us want to see the picture on the front of the box first, so we can develop a strategy and make the process faster. How frustrating would it be to be asked to put the puzzle together without seeing the finished product? And yet, that's how many of our work environments are led. Sometimes no one knows what the picture on the box looks like. Even the top leaders go to work every day and work tirelessly on assembling their version of the puzzle, even though they may have never seen or even asked to see the final image.

Others of us have worked in environments where a privileged few are allowed to look at the box. They may have weekly meetings where they gather around the box and then are instructed to return to their teams to explain and describe the picture on the box. But the end result may be hindered by a lack of focus, time, communication skills, or accountability, and the team never fully understands the big picture.

For team members, assembling the puzzle seems random and meaningless. Motivation runs out over time because there is no reward, people become disgruntled because they are frustrated and confused, threat increases, creativity and innovation fade, and talent leaves.

Seeing the box—the end result or the big picture—matters. When asked why people choose a selected career path or stay loyal to a job, they frequently say it's because they believe they contribute to a meaningful purpose. A common reason for remaining in a career or job is that people feel they have the opportunity to make a difference and to be a part of something greater than themselves.

In 2017, Gallup released a study explaining how millennials want to work and live. One of the key findings was that millennials are among the least engaged generation in the workforce. Only 29% of those interviewed indicated that they were engaged, emotionally and behaviorally, in their job. Another 16% were described as actively disengaged, which means they are out to harm their companies. So, clearly over half are just "showing up." One reason for this level of disengagement, lack of loyalty, and constant job-hopping is that they are looking for a job that "feels worthwhile." The study clearly shows this generation is seeking more than a paycheck; they are seeking a purpose.

Relevant environments provide purpose. One of my healthcare clients excels in providing purpose. In talking about their work, leaders and team members alike frequently use the word "calling" and "sacred vocation." They have a vision to be the most trusted place in giving and receiving safe, quality, and compassionate healthcare. Members of the environment actively hire people whose values align with that vision, speak about the vision in the day-to-day operations, and hold each other accountable for living out that vision. The picture on the proverbial box is compelling, and it unites the entire organization.

When I work with leaders and organizations, one of the first questions I ask is, "What is your vision?" A vision and a vision statement are more than words on a page. Yes, it gives a clear direction for the whole, but it also allows each part to know how they must work together and what role they play in forming the whole. In puzzle terms, it lets the individual pieces know how they must connect to other pieces and clarifies if they are a framing puzzle piece or a center puzzle piece. In other words, a vision facilitates clarity and collaboration.

When establishing a vision, a group of people are deciding what they want to have and what they want to do. That's important, of course. But we need to go beyond what we want to do and have. In my experience, organizations place too much emphasis on writing goals and objectives, even if they meet the SMART criteria (Specific, Measurable, Actionable, Realistic, and Timebound). Goals and objectives, what we want to do and have, are important to be sure. But vision moves us beyond these concepts and encourages us to think about who we want to BE in order for us to do and have those desired things.

This is true at an organizational level, as well as an individual one. I have led several vision-setting retreats, and they are really powerful times when teams or individuals step out of the distractions of the world for a little while to reflect on what they want to do, what they want to have, and who they want to be, with the aid of vision boards. Most people enter the retreat with a relatively clear idea of what they want to do and have; and they think that's what we will be focusing on. Wrong. The hard work, the real, game-changing work, is defining who they will need to BE in order for those things and achievements to happen in the first place.

Vision provides clarity for the whole. It motivates people to strive for something of purpose. Vision guides how the whole leads the parts, and how the parts must align to contribute to the whole. Vision defines what an organization is all about, what it stands for, and what it values. But, equally important, vision brings light to the non-negotiables, the actions and behaviors it will not tolerate, and the activities it must cut. It is as much about letting go as it is about doing more.

Inspiring purpose through a relevant, vision-centered environment not only leverages whole-to-parts, but it also turns the dial to the station everyone is tuned into: WII-FM (What's In It For Me), which activates the brain's reward system. Perhaps out of everything covered in this chapter, this may be the most important reason of all to incorporate relevance. WII-FM—or as someone recently shared, WITT (What's Important To Them)—is the station that triggers the brain's "so what?" system. Think about how successful advertising either directly or indirectly answers the burning question, "So what?" (What's In It For Me?)

Consider how powerful this is in getting us to change and getting us to buy. We purchase stuff to look prettier, younger, sexier, skinnier, stronger, darker, lighter, smarter, taller, and shorter. We want stuff that makes life faster, slower, more exciting, more predictable, less stressful, simple, and complicated. We want more happiness, more adventure, more joy, more calm—want, want, want. Good or bad, it's important to recognize that when we need to lead, influence, and motivate people, we must remember they are tuned into the #1 station on the planet: WII-FM. And that means we need to lead with relevance.

I heard a speaker say recently, "Sell the destination, not the plane." People are either wanting off Pain Island or they are wanting onto Pleasure Island. They don't really care about the boat or the plane that is going to get them there. Think about the last time you thought about going on vacation to a tropical island. Likely you were fixated on leaving behind the stress, problems, and mundane tasks of daily life and eagerly thinking about the food, the drink, the relaxation, the beauty, and the feeling you would have when you reached your tropical destination. Most likely you were not concerned about the fuel capacity or dimensions of the seats on the plane. Of course, you wanted to get there safely, but you weren't concerned with the make, model, and specs of your transportation. Your brain was seeking relief and reward.

Let's apply that to most of the ways leaders present changes or new concepts to their team. Our default is to disregard the WII-FM or WITT, and focus on WITTO (What's Important To The Organization). I remember when one of my clients wanted coaching around how to lead his team in "buying into" a new process. The presentation he created was typical...and so wrong.

The process itself was fabulous; it was proven to drastically reduce waste in terms of errors and time. It also could help the team work more collaboratively and efficiently with fewer problems and hassles. But, did he plan to share any of that information in his presentation? No. He completely overlooked Pain Island and Pleasure Island in creating a 60-minute, 85-slide PowerPoint presentation about the plane.

My recommendation was that he spend no time on talking about the plane until he had communicated, with impact, how his solution was going to take them away from the rocky cliffs of Pain and deliver them to the sandy shores of Pleasure. In fact, I wanted him to build up the team's image of Pain and Pleasure with such clarity and accuracy that they would be begging him to talk about the plane.

Strengths-centered

In addition to being big-picture oriented and vision-centered, relevant environments are strengths-centered. We've established that the brain works most efficiently when we build on familiar, existing neural networks. We've acknowledged that the prefrontal cortex is a priceless treasure that allows us to live our best life. We've confirmed that when threat steps on the scene, the prefrontal cortex goes down. We've established that activating the brain's reward system can enhance performance. We capitalize on all of these brain facts when we engage in and utilize our strengths. Relevance is important to the brain because it is about intentionally identifying and building on strengths.

I believe we are all wonderfully and fearfully made with unique, "set-apart" styles for unique, "set-apart" purposes. In fact, my business scoreboard has, at the top, "Sherry—God gave you a message and a style He did not give to anyone else on the planet. Stand in your value and purpose." I wrote this message to myself so I would focus on my strengths, not my gaps, and so I wouldn't compare myself to the multitude of other insanely talented people in the world.

As my friend repeatedly tells me, "Sherry, stay in your lane."

I can't say that I have altogether stopped worrying about my weaknesses or comparing myself to others, but I can say I'm much better when I read that message on my scoreboard.

I not only believe we are wonderfully and fearfully made because of my own personal values, but I also believe it because that's what science tells us. Your brain is as unique as your fingerprint and is always changing. We all have strengths, and we all have differences. For example, I will never have to answer the question, "Were you a runway model?" I will never be inconvenienced with, "Excuse me, can you put this on the top shelf for me?" No one will ever ask me to do their year-end taxes.

I'm short, I suck at math, I can't grow plants, I'm not a good cook, and I couldn't get a basketball through the net if my life depended on it. My list of "gaps" would grow quite long if I continued to list them. If I lived a life that centered on all that I couldn't do, I would not utilize my prefrontal cortex, I wouldn't build on existing neural networks, and I would live in a constant state of threat, which would impact not only my mental health but also my physical health. All of my "try" would run out. I've lived that life; some of you have, too.

Just the opposite happens, however, when we build a life around our strengths. As one of my coaching clients said when she switched to a job that highlighted her strengths, "I feel like I came alive again."

I love that word: alive. My client's threat was drastically reduced, which lowers negative chemicals like cortisol and increases good chemicals like dopamine. Her prefrontal cortex turned on, allowing her to be her best self and stand in the value of who she truly is. She utilized existing neural networks that allowed her brain to process more effectively and efficiently.

Think on this: if I ask you to write your name with your non-dominant hand, could you do it? Likely yes, you could, but it would be painstaking and of low quality. Writing with your dominant hand, however, makes the process efficient with much better results. The same thing happens when we work with the brain's strengths.

While leaders in a relevant environment ensure how each job fits to produce the whole, they also purposefully ensure each puzzle piece is in the right place and in the right puzzle. In other words, they consciously decide if people are plugged into the positions that highlight their strengths and capitalize on their passions. In his book *Good to Great*, Jim Collins uses the famous bus metaphor that perhaps captures this thought best. He says a strengths-centered culture gets the right people on the right bus in the right seats. Sadly, this choice to be strengths-centered is rare in many areas of our life.

Gallup has done a phenomenal job in helping us better understand engagement and get a read on the percentage of people who are truly engaged at work. Out of Gallup's work, spanning more than 30 years and focusing on millions of people, we better understand how to assess and increase engagement. Through Gallup, the world was introduced to the concept of strengths-based leadership and given tools on how to assess and implement a strengths-based approach.

In 2013, Gallup conducted a study of engagement involving nearly 2 million people across hundreds of cultures. One of the questions participants were asked was, "Do you get to do what you do best every day at work?" Alarmingly, less than 15% were able to "strongly agree" with that statement. Does that mean 85% of the workforce just spends an average 8 hours a day, 40 hours a week, 2,000-ish hours a year, checking email at home, work, weekends, and vacation, performing jobs they don't even really enjoy? As one of my heroes, Pollyanna, once stated, "Breathing is not living."

I hate to be overly dramatic here, but life is short. If the fact that few people get to do every day what they do best is true, and it appears that it is, no wonder we have road rage and stress-related illnesses.

Recently I was coaching a new client in her mid-50s who was considering leaving her corporate job to go into consulting. She said she was just thinking ahead for retirement. Then, she explained that she defines retirement as that period in her life when she finally gets to do what she loves.

Goodness! To someone with a wild, entrepreneur spirit like me, her words cut like a knife. I wanted to scream, "NO!" What her comment (and the results of multiple studies such as Gallup's) should say to us loud and clear is "We have a human capital crisis!" We are wasting our most precious, valuable resources—our talents, strengths, and universe-ordained purposes!

Q12

Gallup has identified 12 core elements, called the Q12, that are excellent predictors of employee engagement and individual and collective work performance. As you read the 12 questions listed below, consider how each connects to the idea of relevance and of having a vision-centered and strengths-centered culture:

1. Do you know what is expected of you at work?
2. Do you have the materials and equipment to do your work right?

3. At work, do you have the opportunity to do what you do best every day?
4. In the last seven days, have you received recognition or praise for doing good work?
5. Does your supervisor, or someone at work, seem to care about you as a person?
6. Is there someone at work who encourages your development?
7. At work, do your opinions seem to count?
8. Does the mission/purpose of your company make you feel your job is important?
9. Are your associates (fellow employees) committed to doing quality work?
10. Do you have a best friend at work?
11. In the last six months, has someone at work talked to you about your progress?
12. In the last year, have you had opportunities to learn and grow?

While Gallup has helped us realize that the level of engagement has a direct correlation to the quality of business outcomes, they have also helped us realize that focusing on strengths has a direct correlation to engagement.

In one study, when leaders focused on strengths, there was a 73% chance of employees stating they were engaged. When leaders in the organization did not focus on strengths, there was only a 9% chance that employees felt engaged. The impact of engagement on business outcomes is far-reaching. Engaged employees take less time off, contribute more ideas, are more likely to refer talent to the organization, have better quality of work, and contribute to a healthier environment for the team.

A relevant, strengths-centered culture identifies individual strengths and interests to make sure that each person is a "fit" with the job and the culture. Focusing on strengths impacts the selection and management processes. It identifies the competencies and skills people need to be successful in their role within that culture. These cultures continuously assess strengths and interests, and delegate accordingly. They consciously listen to what makes someone "come alive," then identify ways for each person to use his or her passion in a positive way for the good of the individual as well as the organization. The result of focusing on strengths is not only increased engagement but also extraordinary business results.

One of my clients has taken this idea of relevance to heart and put action to her beliefs. She identified the key competencies critical for success in all levels of leadership in the organization. From that, she built a roadmap, a big picture or visual of where one is and what he or she would need to develop to advance his or her career.

She invested the time, effort, and money creating a custom-interview process, which all her leaders are trained to conduct. They learn to analyze current and future needs of the job, identify critical competencies for success, and design interview questions using behavioral interviewing techniques. And it's all done with an eye on aligning with the organization's overall vision and values.

Once her organization has the right people on the bus, they make sure everyone is in the right seat. Because demands are ever changing, this must be a continuous process. So throughout the year, her leaders have ongoing formal and informal conversations with team members about their strengths, passion, interests, aspirations, and personal attributes.

With that information, the leaders seek ways to delegate authority, not just tasks, and to align with the individual's strengths and development interests. Leaders deliberately seek ways to make sure employees are connected to people, are plugged into positions, and are involved in projects that capitalize on their interests, natural abilities, and desired career plan.

All my client's team members have an individual development plan, one that is set apart from performance management and lives up to its name. The process begins by an authentic, purposeful conversation where the leader assumes the role of a genuine coach. In this strengths-discovery conversation, leaders do not promise promotion; they simply stay curious and listen with big ears, as we say in the coaching world. The leader guides the conversation with powerful questions in four specific categories: the employee's strengths, aspirations, attributes, and experiences, and then listens attentively.

A few of the sample questions from a strengths-discovery session are:

Strengths

- When people come to you for help, what types of questions are they asking?
- What would your peers identify as your greatest strengths?

Experience

- What prior experiences have prepared you for what you want to do in the future?
- In your current position, what have been the most meaningful experiences?

Aspirations

- If you could create a new position within this organization, what would that look like?
- In two years, what kind of environment do you want to be in? What kind of people do you want to work with? What would a typical day look like?

Attributes

- What can you keep talking about even when you are completely exhausted?
- What comes easily for you?

The leader and team members then work together to establish individual goals, which again are not part of the performance review process and may or may not be related to the team member's current position. Once established, the leader's responsibility is to create a supportive environment for growth, mentor and coach as needed, support as requested, and connect the team member with resources within the company. The leader's responsibility is not to parent, helicopter, or become co-dependent. It is the individual's development plan; therefore, the individual team member is expected to take ownership of the goals and the steps needed to reach those goals. The results of these conversations help leaders to delegate thoughtfully, create succession plans strategically, facilitate networks intentionally, increase engagement exponentially, and reduce the wrong type of turnover dramatically.

Another one of my clients was leading a strengths-discovery session with one of his customer service reps. During the conversation, the service rep said she aspired to move from sales to the training department because she felt energized when facilitating large groups. Once the leader explored further, he learned the team member had occasionally facilitated classes in her last position at a previous organization. Her current job involved talking on the phone with customers one-on-one. So, her leader reached out to contacts in the training department and identified an opportunity. A team was looking for people willing to periodically facilitate new-hire orientation.

Now, this sales rep co-facilitates the orientation once a quarter. She walks into a room with several hundred people and utilizes her passion and strength as a trainer.

Is she a happy, engaged, and motivated team member? She certainly is. Her leader helped her find a way to leverage a strength and a past successful experience to fulfill an aspiration. Best of all, she didn't have to leave her position or organization to exercise her strength.

Another powerful example occurred in an organization I consulted with, where the overall workforce was aging, the company was making deep cuts, and forced retirements and subsequent retirement parties became the norm. Over the year of my engagement with them, I consumed more retirement cake than I care to admit. (I think I've established my love for cake.)

As you can imagine, with cutbacks resulting in forced retirements, morale was low and disengagement was high. Managers came to workshops with specific questions around how to motivate staff. It was not uncommon for people to introduce themselves in ways such as, "Hi, my name is Susan. I'm retiring in 22 months, 4 days, 3 hours, and 32 seconds."

Ever been there? It's a tough crowd. How do you motivate the chronically unmotivated?

One of the managers I coached decided he needed to build relevance, giving people purpose through vision and leveraging their strengths and passions. He conducted strengths-discovery sessions similar to the one I described earlier. Initially, the conversations were rather empty and cynical. A typical response to, "What would you identify as your greatest strength?" was, "I keep my mouth shut."

Or when asked, "What is your top aspiration?" the answer might be, "To get the hell out of here." You get the idea.

This manager, however, persevered. In the discovery conversations, he asked questions and did a lot of listening. He asked people like Susan to share stories and memories. He asked them to talk about leaders, good and bad, whom they had worked for in the company and how those leaders had impacted their lives. He asked them to describe the part of the company's legacy they most wanted to preserve.

From those conversations, the leader and his team created a legacy brown-bag series. For 30 minutes once a week, team members shared their stories and memories with attendees who ranged from retiring employees to those just beginning. They shared how things used to be and what caused it to change, lessons learned, mistakes made, and wins accomplished. They talked about the kind of character and resolve displayed during times of change and uncertainty.

As they shared stories of previous cutbacks, colleagues lost to illness, and the nuances and quirks of previous leaders, they also helped create a bold vision for the future. For those soon-to-retires, they transformed the time they had left with the company. What could have been a meaningless countdown to retirement became a heartfelt time of passing the baton to the next generation. Morale improved, engagement increased, and the culture today is richer because of those legacy brown-bag sessions. Thirty minutes a week transformed those workers who were about to retire. They were no longer just hanging on to draw a paycheck until time ran out.

They had purpose. There was relevance.

So, am I saying that a strengths-focus means never addressing weaknesses? Am I saying that team members should never have to perform a job they don't want to perform? Absolutely not!

I know these questions came to mind for some of you because I have worked with adults for a long time. Once, I was conducting coaching classes at various military bases. One of the classes had a group of shift supervisors for the base's Burger King. I'll never forget the third-shift supervisor leaning back in his chair, arms folded, head tilted back and to the side, and squinting at me with distrust.

He stopped me as I talked about strengths and said in a slow, deep, "been-around-a-long-time" voice, "Well, somebody's got to clean the grill."

So true.

We can never disregard common sense. It's true: in every job there is a "grill" to clean...or a printer cartridge to be replaced, or refrigerators to stock, or trash to be taken out, or budgets to be finalized...and so forth. A strengths-centered focus is not about saying people should never leave their comfort zone or do a job they don't wholeheartedly enjoy. A strengths-centered focus is simply about being intentional to match strengths and interests to the tasks as much as possible.

In addition, a strengths-focus is never about ignoring gaps and weaknesses. Let's face it: we all have gaps and weaknesses, and we have to address those and improve where we can to the best of our ability. A strengths-focus simply means we spend the majority of our effort and energy trying to do what we do best and love. It means we don't wait until we retire or reach a certain age to do what we were designed to do. It means that we work to close gaps and build weaknesses by leveraging strengths. It means we pay more attention on how to better utilize strengths and talents than dwell on the areas where we struggle or do not find purpose.

Greg's story

Let's return a moment to Greg. Greg, you'll recall, was a 26-year employee in a defense manufacturing company where he was the last person to inspect a particular part. The training team I led came one Wednesday morning to ask him a few questions to help us build training modules.

When we asked Greg, a subject-matter expert, where the part ultimately went when it left him, he thought for a moment, pointed to the next station, and answered, "It goes to packing."

My heart sank. Why? Because the part Greg last touched was absolutely critical to the accuracy and precision of the javelin missile system.

How might things have been different in Greg's world if his company's culture focused on incorporating relevance, creating an environment that was vision-centered and strengths-centered both individually and collectively? How might Greg's motivation and performance improved had he known the ultimate purpose of his contributions? Do you think it may have made a difference in the quality of his work? Do you think it may have impacted the level of commitment, passion, and enthusiasm he entered and left the building with every day?

What could have been the cascading effect if Greg had known the vision, the collective "so what?" What could have resulted if Greg had known how integral his job was to a greater cause? Perhaps he may have paid closer attention to global decisions, talked about his job proudly with friends and family, inspired talent to join the company, or had innovative ideas to reduce costs or make significant product improvements. Perhaps his enthusiasm may have been contagious, motivating others he influenced at work.

And how might things have been different in Greg's world if his company's culture was one which was not only vision-centered but also strengths-centered? What if his leaders spent time discovering his strengths and his interests in building websites? What if they had provided opportunities to invest that talent and passion in the company rather than in his side job? It's hard to predict all the contributions he may have made, but at a minimum it is quite likely he would have removed his "countdown to retirement" note from his whiteboard. He may have changed the way he viewed coming to work from a means to an end to an end in itself—from paycheck to purpose.

A relevant culture is compelling, motivating, and purpose-driven. It begins with a vision that is clear and inspiring. The "why" is always guiding the "hows." The whole, or big picture, is always communicated and kept front and center, particularly through times of uncertainty and change. Everyone owns the vision and is clear on how they align and contribute. Work, then, is more enjoyable and engaging because all are working collaboratively to achieve a greater purpose. Because the vision is clear, the organization can strategically decide what is no longer working, what needs to continue, and where they need to improve.

The details of fulfilling that vision leverage both individual and collective strengths. Hires are purposeful. Tasks, projects, roles, and responsibilities are a "fit" with strengths and interests. While gaps and weaknesses aren't ignored, all have multiple opportunities to do what they excel at and enjoy.

In a relevant culture, the organization has fewer problems and better results. And best of all, the workforce doesn't have to wait to retire to do what they love.

Action

Cheaper, better, faster applies to a lot of things.
But not to the human brain.

K ristin sits in her car, fifth in line at the coffee house drive-thru. "Come on, people," she moans. She turns off the podcast reaches for her phone and texts her two teenagers to make sure they are awake and getting ready for school. Lost in her cell screen, the car in front moves up in the line and the car behind her honks. She grabs her purse and digs in the side pocket looking for the protein bar she thought she threw in last night. No luck. "What the hell," she thinks as she pulls up to order. "A lemon muffin, please, and a venti mocha." She pauses, thinks about her first meeting, and asks, "Can you add two extra shots, please?"

Action

As Kristin clumsily tackles her coffee and muffin while entering the crowded freeway, her phone rings. It's her boss who has already been in the office more than an hour. She asks if Kristin can forward a meeting invite, which Kristin does, almost rear-ending the car in front of her. Coffee splashes everywhere. Then her 16-year-old son sends her a text telling her he has to be at school early but his 15-year-old sister won't get in the car. Kristin sends an emoji to him and then texts her daughter: "Please get in the car."

Traffic picks up, and Kristin tunes back into her podcast, which features a health and wellness coach talking about the importance of nutrition and fitness. Kristin knows she needs to make changes in her physical health but doesn't really know where to begin. Since she accepted her promotion a year ago, she has packed on 20 pounds, mostly around her midsection.

The new job takes her to corporate headquarters, adding an hour to her commute each day and requiring longer working hours. She let her gym membership expire. As Kristin listens to the podcast, she remembers how much she enjoyed going to the gym each morning with one of her best friends. They not only motivated each other to work out but provided therapy as well, talking through the struggles of being single moms with teenagers. Kristin really misses those conversations.

She thinks about calling her friend that evening, but she knows all too well she won't—who is she kidding?

The real work begins when she gets home. After the day's petty personnel problems, endless meetings, and a brutal commute, Kristin's evening holds fast food, school projects, laundry, dishes, teenage drama, and chaos. She has a stack of books she would like to read one day. But when Kristin finally crawls into bed, she is physically and mentally exhausted.

Overview

Cheaper, better, faster. These are terms that in theory sound incredibly inviting. Who isn't interested in better, higher-quality outcomes with less input in less time at a reduced cost? Cheaper-better-faster is a phrase that is applied to countless industries, from weight loss to banking to car manufacturers. I've even heard the phrase applied to parenting and dating.

Who isn't down for these benefits? Cheaper? Sounds good. Better? You bet. Faster? Bring it! After all, we live in a world where fast is never fast enough and enough is never enough.

Here's the problem. The cheaper-better-faster dream crumbles in light of what we know about the human brain. The theory that all things can be made cheaper, better, and faster—simultaneously—falls to pieces when applied to the most important piece of equipment in this universe. The equipment that drives everything we are, everything we do, and everything we will be is simply not compatible with the cheaper-better-faster school of thought.

Action

The principle of Action captures the dichotomy of the brain. To accept the principle of Action is make friends with rather than resist the brain's limitations. It involves embracing the brain's capabilities and limitations. It's accepting the brain's efficiency and speed with its requirement for rest and reflection; the brain's massive capacity with its demands for balance and processing time; the brain's complexity with its hunger for simplicity. It involves evaluating when less really is more, surrendering to the brain's unlimited potential and its physical limitations.

In cultures that ignore the Action principle:

- Performance and productivity matter more than the overall health and well-being of the workforce.
- Quantity of results is valued at the expense of an overall quality life.
- Employees' work lives trump their personal lives.
- The rule is, "Leave your personal problems at home."
- Short-term achievement is more important than long-term health and wellness.
- Resources and development are targeted at what can be accomplished for the organization rather than what can assist in helping individuals live their best lives.
- Goals and objectives are measured, but an individual's health markers are not.
- Flexibility is not a concept applied to things like work schedules, locations, and environments.

- Work life and personal life are in two opposite corners.
- One-size-fits-all policies dominate the workplace.
- Long work hours are a badge of success and a sign of achievement.
- Immediate responses to all forms of electronic communication is an expectation whether one is at work, at home, or on vacation.

In contrast, a culture that embraces both the brain's strengths and limitations actively seeks ways to create an environment that provides balance and encourages integration. These environments understand that focus is balanced with rest and one's personal life must align and integrate with one's professional life. The way one brain performs at its best does not apply to everyone. The workforce is composed of highly complex and unique individuals.

In an Action culture:

- Physical space is designed according to how the brain works best.
- People have choices based on how their brains learn and process.
- Policies are uniform but adaptable to certain situations and circumstances.
- The overall health of the organization is measured and monitored as closely as the achievements of the organization.

- Resources are available to employees to receive help, support, and assistance in integrating the demands of work and life.
- Leadership holds everyone to exceptional performance but is open to different ways of achieving that exceptional performance.
- People have opportunities to develop personally and professionally.
- Employees are treated as individuals with unique work styles and needs.
- Individual well-being is just as important as the overall health of the organization's bottom line.

Action cultures realize that cheaper-better-faster may apply to manufacturing cars, streamlining processes, or producing widgets, but it does not apply to the design of the human brain. You may recall Aesop's fable of a Countryman's goose that laid golden eggs. A favorite of mine, this tale is a great reminder of what happens when greed and a scarcity mentality override the natural design and order of things. In an effort to get more golden eggs, the Countryman kills his very source of wealth: his goose. Action cultures are all about golden eggs. But at the same time, they are well aware that people are their greatest resource. So, they take excellent care of the goose.

Reflection

- List 10 activities you performed yesterday. Don't concentrate too hard, just write out the first 10

things that come to mind, such as "checked email."
We will address this later in the chapter.

- What are your top three distractions at work?
  What is the impact of these distractions?
- Of your work habits, which one gives you the best
  results?
- Take a moment to rate the degree with which
  you either agree or disagree with the following
  statements, where 1 means strongly disagree, and 5
  means strongly agree:

	1	2	3	4	5
I can multi-task					
The amount of sleep I get has little impact on my performance.					
A busy lifestyle does not impact my health.					
To promote in my workplace, I must give long hours					
The brain should be treated like any other organ in the body.					

Neurology & Science

For some time, we've heard the rally cry for a work and
life balance. In recent years, experts have realized that we
may be striving for an unachievable goal, and so the cry
changed to work and life integration. I'm not sure I grasp

the difference. In the end, whether we shoot for balance or integration, we are really searching for the way to live our best lives and maximize our potential in every area of our lives.

Oftentimes, it's very difficult to describe when work ends and life begins. I mean, as an entrepreneur, my work is my life's calling. For good or for bad, my life and my work are perfectly blended and one in the same. Most of us are knowledge-workers, which means there isn't a switch in our brain that flips from "work" to "life." We are always doing life while we work and frequently doing work while we live life.

How many of us have spent time on the treadmill mulling over a work-related issue? How often do we have meaningful conversations at work over the similarities or struggles with our spouses, children, and families? And how many of us have gained clarity on a situation at work while we were in the shower or right before we fell asleep? We don't deduct time from our work when we discuss our personal lives. We don't add time to our work when thinking about things related to our work lives on our personal time. So rather than get caught up in whether our work and life are balanced, blended, or integrated, what we are really trying to achieve in the short time we have on the planet, is optimization. We want to optimize who we are in life, and work happens to be one slice of that pie.

In order to live our best lives, we must be our best selves. And in order to do that, we must have and make conscious choices to sustain a great brain. Best-selling author and noted psychiatrist Dr. Daniel Amen has made a profound, though oftentimes controversial, contribution to our understanding how powerful our brain is. His work repeatedly reinforces the thought that our effectiveness in this life is determined by the effectiveness of our brain. If we want to live our optimal best life, our brains must operate at its optimal level.

Most people have never stopped to think about what they must do in order for their brain to work at its optimal level. As a culture, we have adopted practices that are actually brain-antagonistic, such as slamming energy drinks instead of getting a nap. As a workplace, we have adopted assumptions and beliefs that are brain-antagonistic. I would like to debunk five of these myths of optimal brain performance. We'll look at each and how we can do better in the workplace to ignite and optimize each individual in our workforce.

Myth #1: My brain can multitask

To what level do you agree or disagree with this statement? For most of us, especially for those of you who are part of the digital-natives category, the generation of people who have grown up in the digital age, we are wholeheartedly convinced that we are experts at multitasking, that our productivity and quality are not negatively impacted, and that it is insanity to say multitasking is a myth. I mean, if we really believed this fact was a myth, we wouldn't be killing ourselves trying to do it, right? And, our workplaces have completely stopped questioning whether or not multitasking is a myth or an actual ability. In fact, most job descriptions today literally say, "one who can multitask."

So let's take a moment to define what is considered a task and look at what happens in the brain when we attempt to multitask. The mythical phrase, "My brain can multitask," is really "My brain can give equal attention to two attention-rich tasks." The truth is, your brain *cannot* multitask because it can't give equal attention to two attention-rich tasks. Can you chew gum and walk? Most of us can because these two tasks are not competing for processing time and space in the brain. Can you text and walk? Well, there is plenty of video footage to show we can't. (Fortunately, my tripping over a bush while texting and walking one afternoon was not caught on tape.)

The brain has an elaborate attention network. And thousands of studies in the area of multitasking conclude that the brain's complex attention system can only devote resources to one attention-rich task at a time. So, researchers believe that we aren't truly multi-tasking at all. The brain's attention system is not devoting resources to multiple tasks simultaneously; rather, it appears the brain is simply switching from task to task at lightning speed.

"So what," you ask?

Well, as a friend of mine once said, "I don't care how the brain handles all that I'm expected to do as long as it gets handled and I keep my job and people off my back."

Valid point. The problem is that rapidly switching back and forth is not how the brain works best, and when we do so, there are costs and consequences.

Multitasking interferes with our efficiency. When we multitask, or suffer from an interruption, it simply takes us longer to return to the task we were previously doing, if we actually ever return to it at all. Some studies indicate the return time to the original task can be as high as 25 minutes. Studies have also shown multitasking can result in up to a 50% increase in errors and a 40% decrease in productivity. This isn't hard to believe when you consider the energy and focus required in restarting, losing momentum, and subsequently working with increased stress and fatigue.

Multitasking interferes with our overall performance. In one study, albeit a controversial one, those who were distracted by multitasking and suffered from multiple interruptions throughout the day, experienced a decline in IQ more than twice that of those who smoke marijuana. The study has sparked controversy because multitasking and marijuana have a host of other different types of effects on the brain. But the point is that multitasking impacts our ability to perform at our optimum level.

Multitasking impacts performance because it affects how and where information is learned and stored in the brain. It appears multitasking causes information to be stored in the "wrong" part of the brain. When we multitask, we store information in the striatum, a part of the brain. dedicated to procedure and skills rather than facts and ideas. When we focus and prioritize our attention, information is stored in the hippocampus, a part of the brain critical for long-term memory and synthesizing new information with existing information.

Finally, multitasking—that treasured, elusive ability—depletes the prefrontal cortex of energy and activates the reward system. This is particularly important to note. Remember all of the priceless functions of the PFC from the chapter on Challenge? One of those important functions came in several forms of self-control, such as emotional, financial, cognitive, and perspective self-control. Increased PFC activity means a rise in these abilities. Conversely, decreased activity in the PFC means a decline in these abilities, leading to less self-control and more impulsiveness. Couple that with the fact multitasking activates the brain's reward system in an addictive kind of way, almost like a craving. The result is a brain that gets a "feel-good" reward from multitasking and acts impulsively to do more of it. So in a sense, the thinking part of the brain is hijacked, and we fully embrace the multitasking frenzy. Therefore, we get a high or a charge out of busy brain activity.

Many of us feel the withdrawals of this addiction when we are away from the busy action of our daily lives, such as when we are on vacation. We simply don't know what to do with ourselves because of our addiction to being busy. So, setting a higher standard in our multitasking-obsessed workforce is to pass on hiring the candidate who self-proclaims he or she can multitask. Rather, the more exceptional hire would be the candidate with the presence of mind to unitask.

Myth #2: I don't need sleep

I led a retreat once where I discussed ways to care for the brain. One of those suggestions was go to sleep. One executive talked with me at every break adamantly proclaiming he only needed two hours of sleep a night. So, was his assertion accurate, or is he living in a state of deception and denial? To what degree did you agree or disagree with the statement, "I don't need sleep?"

I'm claiming this belief a myth because sleep is so integral to optimal performance. In fact, one of the best things we can do to optimize performance and integrate the principle of Action in our environment is turn it off and go to sleep.

One of the reasons I love studying the brain is because the more we learn and think we "know," the more we are humbled by what we don't know. For example, how much sleep do we need? Like many of you, I grew up hearing we need anywhere between seven-10 hours of sleep, and that is definitely true for me. I often tell people I have the gift of sleep and have always needed more sleep than most of my peers and family members in order to be my best. But recent research in the area of sleep, indicates this seven-10 hour standard may not be a one-size-fits-all. In fact, that executive may not have been in denial, he may have been telling the truth. Though rare, he may only need two hours.

Action

In 2015, the National Sleep Foundation conducted an extensive study to re-evaluate sleep recommendations. Among their conclusions was that the "standard" sleep requirement varies from person to person across our lifespans. And while there is a "normal" range of sleep time, meaning the amount of time for the average person to feel healthy and well-rested, there are deviations from the norm. So, the key is to determine what sleep time is optimal for you and to be vigilant in protecting that time.

A second question of mystery about the brain, then, is, "Why do we sleep?" In years past, we thought the reason the brain needed sleep was to rest, reboot, learn, recharge, or dream. But in reality, we really don't know why the brain needs sleep. One of the most plausible reasons why sleep is critical to optimal performance because this is a time when the brain actively processes and stores information and experiences. One of my professors once shared that the brain does things for us at night that it simply won't do any other time; one of those is efficiently process information and memories.

Earlier I mentioned the part of the brain called the hippocampus, located in the medial temporal lobe of the brain. Through the years, I have heard the hippocampus called the 'fortress of human memory' and the brain's 'surge protector.' Because this part of the brain is so important, and because sleep is so vital to it working correctly, take a closer look at what the hippocampus does for us and how its functions can be a predictor of optimal performance.

Unforgettable Leadership

Ever crammed the night before the test? I remember driving to an exam one time and avoiding everyone I knew. I was afraid if I talked to them, the facts and dates I had memorized might leak out of my brain. I was holding these facts in the tank. After the test, a loud flushing sound was heard throughout the campus. It was the sound of me flushing the facts out of my head. I think I did fine on the test, but my cramming the night before did not result in long-term, deep-down-in-my-bones kind of learning.

Here's why.

If new information is like a large pitcher of water, the hippocampus is like a small cup. For real learning, at least two things must happen. First, we must be exposed to the information, hopefully in an environment and with a delivery method that is brain-friendly. Then the brain requires time to sort, file, and delete that information. When does the brain sort, file, and delete? You guessed it: when we sleep.

The hippocampus does its best work when we sleep. In fact, it performs important functions critical to learning and memory that it simply can't do any other time. The challenge is that the consequences of lack of sleep don't show up in one's life immediately. It's sort of like eating ice cream before you go to bed every night; its effect on your waistline may not appear instantly, but it will eventually show up in a big way. The same is true with sleep. When we don't monitor our rest and subsequently get enough of it, we accrue a sleep debt.

Action

Studies have shown that the effects of a sleep debt can begin to appear within two weeks of getting less than six hours of sleep each night. The effects can be relatively mild, such as irritability, memory laps, memory loss, and reduced alertness. But the effects can also be life-threatening, increasing the chances of serious conditions such as Type 2 diabetes, heart disease, cancer, Alzheimer's disease, and hallucinations. An estimated 100,000 accidents on the road each year are caused by sleep-deprived drivers.

The problem is that a sleep debt impairs our judgment. When our judgement is impaired, we can no longer accurately assess whether or not we have a sleep deficit. We may not recognize or acknowledge the impairments resulting from our deficit. So we keep pushing forward to finish the project or drive the car. In that sense, the executive mentioned earlier, the one who believed he only needs two hours of sleep a night, may have been delusional and operating under a sleep debt. Additionally, like any debt, it takes time to pay it back. We simply can't operate on little sleep for weeks and expect to pay it all back by sleeping in on a Saturday morning.

Not only is sleep important at night, but many studies indicate the benefit of bringing sleep into the day. The reason is because the body seems to have a natural craving for sleep at least twice in a 24-hour period. The primary craving hits between midnight and 7 a.m., and the second occurs in the afternoon, usually between 1-4 p.m. The National Sleep Foundation says that a nap of 20-30 minutes during the day can improve mood, alertness, and performance. It is rumored that many high performers through the years—such as Thomas Edison, Napoleon, Ronald Reagan, and John F. Kennedy—were known to leverage the power of naps. I'm personally a big fan of naps.

Napping, of course, has been a socially-accepted and even a socially-expected practice in many countries for centuries. For whatever reason, however, they haven't always been welcome in America. In fact, for most Americans, running on little to no sleep is often worn like a badge of honor, and stopping to take a nap is perceived as a sign of laziness. It's time to bust this myth. Your brain needs sleep.

Myth #3: I am not making myself sick

It's interesting how easy it is to blame outside forces and other people on making us sick. We cite everything from vaccinations and pollution to cleaning solutions and McDonald's. But the truth is, we are making ourselves sick. In fact, the Centers for Disease Control estimate that as much as 85% of our medical expenditures are tied directly or indirectly to stress-related illnesses. Other studies, targeting the workforce specifically, estimate that workplace stress is causing anywhere from $190 to $300 billion annually. With healthcare costs increasing and healthcare coverage decreasing at an alarming rate, we have to stop blaming external forces for our stress-related illnesses and look in the mirror. WE are making ourselves sick.

Action

Why does stress, and a lack of attention to the Action principle in our lives, make us sick? The brain is directly connected to your immune system. This is the anatomical reason why, when we are under negative stress for long periods of time, we have a much higher risk of becoming sick. It's no mystery. In fact, when we are under negative stress, we should expect our health to fail and shift into becoming a self-caretaking machine! When we are stressed, we experience elevated levels of cortisol, a stress hormone that impacts memory, sleep, and weight. In fact, one of my mentors describes cortisol as the hormone that makes us "fat, sleepy, and stupid."

Multiple studies have demonstrated that anxiety-reducing practices that reduce cortisol, such as yoga and mindfulness meditation, result in enhanced sleep and clarity of thought as well as decreased waist sizes, particularly in women. Cortisol also slows the body's healing process because it disrupts the immune response. This hormone, in appropriate levels, turns off inflammation in the body. However, when excessive levels of cortisol exist over time, the body becomes desensitized and inflammation dramatically accelerates. Long-term, chronic inflammation damages blood cells and brain cells leading to a multitude of illnesses. Changes in life situations, even good changes, increase the likelihood we will be sick.

I recall the first time I completed the Life Change Index Scale, also known as the Holmes and Rahe Stress Scale or the Social Readjustment Rating Scale (SRRS). In 1967,

Holmes and Rahe wanted to see if stress had a connection to illness. They surveyed more than 5,000 medical patients by asking them to indicate whether they had experienced, within the previous two years, 43 life events. A value, or Life Change Unit (LCU), was assigned to negative and positive life events. For example, divorce gets a value of 73 points, while marriage gets a value of 50 points. Marital reconciliation, a seemingly positive event, receives a higher LCU than personal injury, a seemingly negative event. The higher the total score, the greater the likelihood of illness.

I joked as I filled out the survey. I added my points, checked the scale, and saw that I had an 80% chance of illness. In two weeks, I was in the hospital; it turns out that this scale was an excellent predictor of illness. In fact, in one study, the U.S. military used it to accurately estimate how many people would visit the ship infirmary while on a six-month deployment.

Stress, particularly in situations which we perceive as negative and out of our control, takes a toll on our performance, our health, and our life. In the book "Margin," Dr. Richard Swenson tells the story of Ignaz Semmelweis, a 19th-century surgeon who practiced before the discovery of microbes. He simply made an observation: physicians who moved from performing autopsies in the morgue to treating patients in the postpartum ward were killing patients. He was one of the first to consider the possibility that there could be invisible killers on physicians' hands. Semmelweis advocated hand-washing with chlorinated lime after performing the autopsies, and after that step was put into action, deaths in the postpartum ward stopped. One would think he would have been hailed a hero, but not so. Semmelweis was crucified by the medical community because he suggested doctors were causing the deaths. In his book, Swenson powerfully compares microbes to overload: overload is also an invisible killer.

Myth #4: Long hours equals a promotion

Just like in Kristin's story, leaders often are in the office long before their team arrives and long after they leave. While their intentions may be to model commitment and work ethic, they are oftentimes modeling unhealthy work habits and a lack of boundaries, and are subtly sending the message to the team that long hours is what it takes if they, too, want to get ahead. And, when we are at the office, we can't be other places that are important to a healthy life balance. Even leaders have not figured out how to be in two places at once.

When we look to the brain, however, we see that it only has so much cognitive energy it can expend during a given period of time. The prefrontal cortex burns an enormous amount of fuel. In fact, while the brain makes up only 2% of your total body, it consumes 20% of the oxygen you breath and 20% of the energy we take in from food. Much like your vehicle's gas tank, your cognitive fuel eventually runs down to empty. With every cognitively-demanding decision we make, we deplete fuel and energy reserves in the PFC.

Dr. David Rock, author of *Your Brain at Work*, offers a different metaphor. He compares the PFC to a small stage in a small theater. The stage can only hold a few actors (things from our inner thoughts or outer world that demand conscious thought), and it requires a great deal of lighting (energy). As the light/energy dims, we lose the ability for the "actors" to perform. In other words, as the energy wanes, so does the priceless function of the PFC. This means that the brain has limitations, and we cannot be "on" at full capacity 24/7.

Brain Rules, the brilliant and practical book by John J. Medina, is accompanied by several videos. In the video on "Attention," Medina features a consultant who reaffirms that those organizations who believe they are always "on" are actually those organizations that are always distracted and inefficient. Longer hours don't necessarily translate into a stronger work ethic, greater performance, or higher productivity. Longer hours may simply equal longer hours. It's likely that the person staying longest at the office is the least efficient, and possibly the least productive, worker.

Myth #5: The brain is unlike anything else

Admittedly, this myth is tricky. Of course your brain is not like anything else in your body—it's your brain. And clearly, if you remove it, the liver isn't going to take over its functions. In many respects, your brain is unique, but in other aspects, your brain is just like your heart, your lungs, or the bones in your leg. It requires proactive healthcare and commitment to wellness to function at its best.

Action

It's time we all wake up to the critical issue of mental health. At some point in our lives, most of us will either personally—or by way of a close family member, close friend, or coworker—experience the impact of a mental health problem. The percentage of people who will experience a mental health challenge in their lifetime is predicted to be around 50%. It is high time we remove the stigma associated with this issue. A brain problem is no different from a heart malfunction, lung condition, or broken leg. And just like with these obstacles, the right intervention can improve the issue, while the wrong (or no) intervention can spell disaster.

A brain problem is a physical problem, not a character problem. You wouldn't attempt to will yourself out of having a heart attack; you would seek help from professionals who understand that organ. In the same way, we can't will ourselves out of a mental-health dilemma. We need to seek professionals who understand that precious structure. Even if society didn't stigmatize seeking help, many doctors who treat brain problems—a.k.a. mental health issues—never look at the actual organ they are treating.

One reason I am an avid admirer of Dr. Daniel Amen is because he has led the charge in actually looking at the brain, seeing what is working too hard and not hard enough, and providing the right intervention. Unfortunately, we have a long way to go in this area. I can speak to this personally, having lived with someone with an addicted brain. We invested our hope, our time, and thousands of dollars on psychiatrists, counselors, physicians, and rehab centers; not one professional we visited over the course of at least 10 years ever actually looked at the organ they were treating, the source of the problem. Repeatedly, we were given prescriptions for medications and told, "Come back in six weeks, and let's see how you are doing."

Six weeks! Are you kidding? In the life of someone suffering with a mental illness and their families, six weeks can seem like a lifetime. Even more, six weeks can be the end of a lifetime.

In addressing any other health problem, not looking at the organ one is treating might be called malpractice. I often wondered what these doctors would have done if I had brought my family member in with a broken foot. Would they simply have given us medications with instructions to come back in six weeks to see how the foot was feeling and healing? No, they would have taken X-rays to see the bone fracture and likely applied a cast or performed surgery.

Amen has been revolutionary in that he has had the audacity to ask those in the mental health business to look at the organ they are treating. And he has raised awareness among those suffering the consequences of mental illness to demand better treatment.

With the right intervention in the right situation, the brain can heal itself and get better; this is called neuroplasticity. So a brain problem is not a hopeless problem. People with mental health challenges simply need to access the right help; as they heal, their performance improves and their lives get better, as do the lives of all of those around them who are impacted by the illness.

Application

Let's take a look at how we can turn these myths to truths and apply them in practical ways to ignite the workforce and live an optimal life. There are practical ways we can implement the principle of Action in our personal lives and the lives of our organizations. As best-selling author Gretchen Rubin has helped us to realize, it's all about habits.

If we want our lives to change, we must change our habits. If your habits involve being distracted and reactive, caught in the reward cycle of multitasking, maybe it's time to adopt some new ones.

Rubin shows us in her book, *Better than Before*, that habits are not one-size-fits-all. Every person is different, and every organization is different. So as I discuss these truths and accompanying productive habits, I challenge you to consider how to adapt them to work best for you, your team, and your organization.

Truth #1: My brain can unitask

If the multitasking brain is distracted, then the unitasking brain is focused. If the multitasking brain is reactive, then the unitasking brain is proactive. In workshops, I love to contrast the work habits of most

Americans with those of high performers and MacArthur Fellows who have received a "genius" grant. The prestigious genius grant is designed to, as its website states:

> ...encourage people of outstanding talent to pursue their own creative, intellectual, and professional inclinations...(and) to advance their expertise, engage in bold new work, or, if they wish, to change fields or alter the direction of their careers...to enable recipients to exercise their own creative instincts for the benefit of human society.

The work habits of most Americans can be described by highly distracted and reactive. The average American's life is dominated by interruptions and distractions in the form of people and of things that buzz and pop up. We check our email constantly, even on vacation, and are slaves to the screen. I am guilty of this myself. A few years ago I arrived at the airport, headed to speak at a conference, and realized I had forgotten my smartphone. Sheer panic ensued. My plane was leaving, and I couldn't drive back home and get my beloved device, which meant I spent the entire weekend phoneless. I was embarrassed at how many times I reached for my phone to check texts or surf social media, only to remember it wasn't there. However, I must admit that breaking away from the device for the weekend was a wonderful gift.

Action

The work habits of high performers and Macarthur Fellows are quite different. Not surprisingly, two of the barriers to both performance and productivity were interruptions and distractions. In Uncommon Genius, Denise Shekerjian explored the common traits of forty winners of the MacArthur award. What she didn't find were people who gave in to distraction and rushing, bouncing around from one unrelated idea and task to another. Rather, what she found was a group committed to a vision with unrelenting focus, purpose, determination, courage, discipline, and commitment over the long haul.

Taking time out to think is a powerful practice. One organization I consulted with took this idea to heart and adopted what they called "the Sacred 60." Each person was allowed and encouraged to take 60 minutes a day to "check out" and redirect their focus. They even went as far as to purchase police crime scene tape, humorously closing off their cubes when they were taking their "Sacred 60"—and their teammates respected their wish for no interruptions.

The idea is simply to disconnect on purpose. Georgetown professor Cal Newport calls this "deep work," and in his book of the same title, he says that the practice is essential to developing and using our greatest levels of intellectual abilities. Deep work requires making an intentional, powerful decision to check out and turn off all of the noise that is distracting us.

I'm a productivity-enhancing junkie and a fan of noted personal development trainer Brendon Burchard, who studies the habits of high performers and encourages reclaiming ownership of our life. Burchard suggests a simple productivity planning tool that I use each day. The planning template includes three P's: projects, people, and priorities. Each morning, I spend about 15 minutes listing my top three projects and three steps I need to take to move the project. I write down the people I need to reach out to and the people I'm waiting on. Then, I list priorities that absolutely must be done for the day. I've added my own fourth P: praise. I find it invaluable to praise. I either highlight three wins or gratitudes or send a praise to someone else who has made my life easier or more fulfilling.

As I stated earlier, the goal of using any habit-changing tip is to make it work for you. However, if you use a planning tool such as the one described above to kickstart your day, Burchard encourages completing your plan before checking your email. Why? Because your email is typically other people's agenda for your day and your life. It's important that we set our agenda before we give that over to anyone else.

Another useful planning tool is one that was popularized by many, including author Stephen Covey. This tool has been called the Time Management Matrix, the Eisenhower Decision Matrix, and the Eisenhower Box. Eisenhower supposedly created this tool that reportedly helped him become the high performer and producer he was. Regardless of when it was created or by whom, this matrix is a powerful tool for reflecting, focusing, and planning, and can be used to plan out a day, a week, a month, or a project.

As the illustration below shows, the matrix or box contains four sections. The horizontal row marks things that are "Important" to you and are vital because they are aligned with your values and goals. The "Not Important" row contains those activities that are not directly aligned with your goals and values. The vertical column marks the "Urgent" tasks, those things that are either screaming for your attention or are time-bound. The "Not urgent" are, of course, those things that are quietly waiting in the background.

	Urgent	Not Urgent
Important	1) Important/Urgent • Quick wins • Emergencies • Deadlines	2) Important/Not Urgent • Major projects • Investing in self & others • Valuable goals
Not Important	3) Not Important/ Urgent • ROPEs • Fill Ins	4) Not Important/Not Urgent • Time wasters • Non-value-added activites

Quadrant 1: Important & Urgent

These are activities that are aligned with our goals and values, and they are time-bound. For example, if, while you were reading this, someone ran into the room bleeding and screaming, I'm certain you wouldn't tell them to wait a second while you finished the page. The incident would demand your immediate attention.

Quadrant 2: Important & Not Urgent

These are vital activities, but they aren't screaming at us—yet—like going to the gym, eating healthy, taking time to invest in a relationship, and completing preventative health screenings. I often talk about Quadrant 2 like fueling your car: you don't always feel like you have time to stop and refuel, but if you don't, you end up on the side of the interstate with much bigger problems.

Quadrant 3: Not Important & Urgent

These activities are important to other people, but they may or may not be important to us. I call this quadrant ROPEs (Responding to Other People's Emergencies). A lot of meetings and projects fall into this category, and it is the primary quadrant for most emails, meetings, and those volunteer opportunities we agree to before actually thinking through the commitment.

Quadrant 4: Not Important & Not Urgent

These are activities that, to put it nicely, are time-wasters. This is often the quadrant of procrastination, social media stalking, endless reality-show watching, and video gaming.

Using the list you created under the Reflection heading earlier in this chapter of 10 activities you performed yesterday, put each one in its appropriate quadrant.

Action

If we were to record all of our activities for a day or a week, ideally the majority would fall into Quadrant 2, the proactive, intentional, power section. The more time we spend in Quadrant 2, the less time we will have in the other three. Our problems decrease, along with those we impose on others, and our results increase.

A few notes about the quadrants:

- Quadrant I activities activate adrenaline and the reward system; in other words, they give us a rush, and it's easy to get addicted to the feeling of being busy.
- Quadrant 1 is often called the "heart-attack quadrant."
- Most things in Quadrant 1 can been avoided if we deal with them responsibly in Quadrant 2.
- Our Quadrant 1 activities become someone else's Quadrant 1 or 3 problem; when we aren't responsible, we impact those around us.
- When you find yourself in Quadrant 4 (i.e., playing multiple games of Candy Crush on your smartphone), ask yourself, "What opportunities in Quadrant 2 am I missing out on?" (i.e., a conversation with your family at the dinner table).

Both the matrix and Burchard's planning tool can be used by an individual, a team, or an organization to plan a project, one day, one week, or beyond. Again, the idea is to take the tool and make it work for your brain and your organization's culture.

In addition to carving out time to think and plan, high performers turn off technology and "just say no" to distractions and interruptions—on purpose (not because you leave for the airport without your smartphone by accident). I jokingly say that my dying words will most likely be, "Where's my phone?" because it's a question I ask entirely too often. As a coach, I've helped many people through the years do the impossible: turn off technology, check email at preselected times (such as at lunch, at the end of the day, or at the top of the hour), set alarms for breathing exercises, make appointments with themselves for focus time, and create technology-free work spaces or "dead zones." I have to discipline myself regularly to implement these practices in my own life.

At first, this change in living and being may be very uncomfortable or even painful. Much like an addict coming off of a drug, the withdrawals from being busy are not pleasant. But soon, a healthier life returns because a healthier brain returns. As one of my clients once told me, "I feel alive again." That's what happens when we trade in cramming, crowding, and chaos for calm.

To better integrate the Action principle into the work culture, let's stop writing "a candidate can multitask" into our job descriptions. Equip team members with tools to plan and focus, and educate them on the habits of high performers. Stop expecting people to respond immediately to every need and flagging every email as high priority. Guide the team in identifying the primary distractors and interruptions, then facilitate the creation of etiquette rules of operation. Allow team members time and work spaces to focus, reflect, collaborate, and plan.

Multitasking and filling our lives to the brim with activity is not an ability but a habit we mindlessly fall into. As Rubin encourages us, we must mindfully choose our habits. When we do, this mindfulness creates a momentum that enhances our energy and our growth. Rather than multitask, I challenge you to unitask.

Truth #2: I need sleep

I coached an executive whose life, like many executives, was on overload. Soon into our sessions, she revealed she was having marital problems. Her husband had told her that he had "had enough" and was tired of being her second priority after work. As we dug deeper, the main problem was that she returned emails before she went to sleep. She would become fully engrossed, one email would lead to another, and she wouldn't go to bed until the early morning hours. Not only did this habit make her husband feel devalued, but she was accruing a serious sleep debt and could no longer deny the effects. The solution? She decided if her alarm could wake her up, it could tell her to go to bed. So, at 9:00 p.m., her alarm goes off. She closes her computer and follows a routine she has created to make sure she is in bed and asleep on time.

Certainly sleep requirements vary among individuals and at different times in our lifecycle. They key is self-awareness and accurate self-assessment. How much

119

sleep are you getting? What is the quality of your sleep? Are you experiencing any symptoms of sleep deprivation? Do you know how much sleep you need to truly feel healthy and rested? And, do the people closest to you agree with how you've answered these questions?

In addition to the primary time the brain needs sleep, how can we honor the brain's secondary time for rest, that period between 1:00-4:00 p.m.? In *Brain Rules*, Medina makes the shocking suggestion to actually take a nap. Daniel Pink, in his book *When*, recommends what he calls a nappuccino, an afternoon coffee followed by a brief nap. Some companies have recognized the value in providing time and space for the the brain to rest. At a minimum, we should schedule less cognitively taxing tasks during the afternoon hours of 1:00-4:00 p.m., or take stretch breaks more frequently.

There is an ebb and flow to our brain's ability to be "on." We need to honor and lean into that rhythm rather than resist it. By getting sleep and scheduling cognitively demanding tasks accordingly, we think better and more efficiently. This cascades into a higher-quality work and personal life. Rather than push through the fatigue, we need sleep and periods of rest and reflection.

Truth #3: You are making yourself sick

Organizations that embrace the Action principle realize our choices and lifestyles have an impact on health. For many years, I consulted with one of the nation's largest providers of medical and health insurance. During that time, they surveyed the physical health of their workforce, measuring and tracking certain health markers such as lifestyle habits, eating habits, weight, body fat, etc. What they learned from the survey was that their company was the most unhealthy organization they insured.

So they began to make changes: no smoking on the property, healthier food choices in the vending machines and cafeteria, walking programs, health education training, and financial incentives for workers to lose weight, reduce body fat, lower cholesterol and blood pressure, and have annual screenings. Within two years, they moved from the unhealthiest to the healthiest company they insured.

Clearly, the choices we make matter; most people know that. Smoking and obesity kills. The food we eat directly impacts our health. Our bodies have more than 650 muscles—we are born to move. But we all know there is a great chasm between knowing and doing. In fact, one of my favorite quotes is, "To know and not to do is not to know."

The great news is that small changes can produce big results. For example, a colleague of mine was part of America on the Move, a national initiative designed to inspire positive lifestyle changes and improve overall health and well-being. She was part of a team that looked at the physical growth of Americans over an extended period of time. What could have prevented this substantial growth? Only 2,000 more steps and 100 calories less a day.

The myth is that we are not responsible for our health.

The comfort in that myth is that we can sit back and blame external forces and not accept responsibility for our own actions and choices. The truth is that we are responsible for our health. If our choices are making us sick, let's make different choices. By doing so, we decrease the likelihood of becoming ill and increase the likelihood of living our best, most productive lives.

Truth #4: Productive hours are rewarded

In Action cultures, long hours at work do not equal promotion; productive hours at work equal promotion. Oftentimes, we believe that because someone is "in the classroom," they are learning. Clearly, someone can be sitting in a room, looking right at a facilitator, and not grasp one word he says. The same is true in the workplace. Just because someone is "in the office" doesn't mean he or she is being productive. Oftentimes, "being at work" means nothing more than "being at work."

We frequently lose sight of boundaries at work. In one organization where I consulted, C-suite, executive leaders worked 24/7 and expected everyone else to do the same. The result of that mentality over time was not increased productivity but rather burn out, cognitive fatigue, and resentment.

Action cultures think differently. They recognize that time spent doesn't always translate into a quality product. I remember listening to one of the finest leaders I've ever coached give direction to one of her team members. She assigned him a project and clearly stated the goals. Then she gave him the authority and trust to determine how many hours were needed to reach the goal.

Action cultures recognize that "the office" is not the only place—and even sometimes the last place—where people are productive. They intentionally ask the question, "Does everyone have to be in the same physical space at the same time to get the job done?" If not, they provide options, allow people choices, trust the team, and keep an eye out for results.

For example, team members at one of my client companies have a variety of choices in their work spaces. Team members have an open cubicle where they can work, or they can choose to schedule private spaces with a door. They can work in the company coffee shop or in collaborative spaces located both inside and outside the building.

Another company allows employees to work in their space of choice as well as during the times that best suit their work habits and needs. One employee I coached works from home from 8:00-10:00 a.m. He then drives to his office building and works from 11:00 a.m.-6:00 p.m. This allows him to avoid rush-hour traffic and reduce his commute each way by 45 minutes. The next time you are sitting in traffic, think about how ridiculous it is that everyone is rushing to work and rushing home from work during the same window of time.

Does it have to be that way? Many organizations I've worked with over the years are 100% virtual. They find people are more productive when they work from home. Certainly, overhead costs drastically go down. They simply use processes and tools to enhance communication and overcome other challenges that can occur in virtual work settings.

In my experience, flexible work spaces and work schedules are simply an issue of trust and questioning foundational beliefs. Action cultures are also Challenge cultures, meaning they operate on trust and not threat. In addition, they don't stop with the belief, "That would never work here." Rather, they ask, "Could that work here? If so, how do we make it happen?"

Truth #5: My brain is like any other organ

Your brain is the driver of everything you do. In *Making a Good Brain Great*, Dr. Amen reveals what he has learned from studying thousands upon thousands of brain scans. One of his key learnings is that the brain influences every part of who we are and what we do from our abilities and talents to our likes and dislikes. We need to come out of the Dark Ages and get to know how our brains work best.

The brain is your most important piece of equipment. Take good care of it. If it is under undue stress, take really good care of it. Consider this: if your job was to lift 200-pound boxes and your back started hurting, you might go see a doctor, get an X-ray, wear a brace, or go on light duty at work. All of those options would be expected and acceptable. In fact, most people would be surprised if you didn't have your back examined and made some adjustments. Few would say, "He just needs to suck it up and think more positively."

The same should be true for the brain. Our job is to be productive and live our best, optimal lives. If we have a brain problem, let's do something about it. Sometimes the solution may be increasing the margin, or bandwidth, in our lives, getting sleep, eating better, exercising more, or rescheduling activities. Sometimes the solution may require medical intervention. And, that's OK, too. The point is, don't ignore the problem (in yourself or others), do nothing, and act shocked when performance and life don't improve.

The brain, like any organ, needs its owner to make certain choices and take certain actions to keep it healthy. And like any organ, the brain can be injured and stop functioning properly. In those instances, get it the help it needs. It's not a willpower problem; it's simply a brain problem. And brain problems, like any other body issue, will get worse with neglect but can improve with the right help.

Kristin is living like the majority of Americans. She assumes that busy is productive, that distracted is normal, and that calm is unachievable. She allows everyone else to dictate the quality of her life. A client I coached was in a situation similar to Kristin's, and he summed it up by saying, "I don't even know who I am or what I want anymore." I've been there. It sometimes takes making tough decisions to move out of that place, but it is absolutely possible. Remember, when it comes to the brain and the quality of life, small changes really can produce big results.

If we want to achieve balance, integration, and optimal lives, we have to follow the framework of how the brain works best and not against it. We must trade beliefs. Rather than thinking that the brain can multitask without consequences, we must strive to unitask. Rather than believing we don't need sleep, we have to tune into the brain's need for a natural rhythm and protect the time we need for sleep. Rather than blaming and betting our health and wellness on outside forces, we need to be vigilant in making healthy choices and living healthy lifestyles.

Rather than equating long hours with high productivity, we need to be mindful of how and where we work best and be open-minded as to how and where work can be done. Let's set aside the need to monitor and micro-manage. The results will always speak. Pay less attention to who's sitting in a chair or in the building and pay more attention to the outcomes they accomplish.

Finally, we need to remove the mystery of the brain. While there is a great deal we need to learn, we know that the brain, like any other part of the body, must be treated with respect and given attention when it is not working properly. Let's put aside the stigma of mental health challenges, for that is often the greatest barrier to getting help and getting better.

Cultures that embrace the Action principle are smart. They pay attention to the brain's needs, strengths, and limitations, and adapt accordingly. It's true that almost everything can be made cheaper, better, and faster—except the human brain.

Novelty

| veering from convention

*Think big. Think different.
Think deep. Think forward.*

"Can you grab my backpack?" Sara asks Tom as they head out to work. It's a familiar routine, and both are grateful to share their commute and have some quality time together each morning. Tom and Sara met in grad school and have been married for almost 18 years. They both work in Information Technology and were employed by the same company until about a year ago, when Sara changed jobs and assumed a new position in the banking industry. Fortunately, her office is only about three miles from Tom's.

"Make it a great day," Tom says as he pulls the car up to Sara's building. She gives him a kiss, grabs her backpack, and walks into her building. Tom makes his way to his office building, finds a parking spot, and checks his social media one last time as he walks in.

Tom flashes his badge to the guard at the security desk who does not acknowledge him. He turns toward a large sign: Innovation Lab. He passes several co-workers who move quickly down the hall, heads down, walking in silence while checking their text messages. The walls around him are impressive, with large letters spelling out the word "innovation" and posters featuring their product and happy customers.

The lab where Tom works has a chic, contemporary appearance. This newly renovated section of the office building was the pet project of their new CEO, who brought in consultants to rebrand the company's image. Innovation was the key message, and this featured word made its way into the company's list of values, the mission statement, signage, and marketing materials.

Tom heads to his open cubicle space, another result of the consultants' efforts to force better communication and collaboration. He puts in his earbuds to concentrate (distraction and noise are already growing around him) and pulls his schedule up on his monitor. His color-coded calendar is so crammed with back-to-back meetings that it looks more like a jar of jelly beans than a schedule.

He sees a new meeting request that has taken over the time he had blocked out for working on the audit report due Friday. The meeting request is to review his annual performance with a leader he has only worked under for three months. Tom is curious how this new leader will write his annual review, seeing that his last leader rarely communicated with him and never gave him performance feedback throughout the year.

Tom's first meeting of the day is about an innovative change in testing that would better support the company's new product line. The project lead begins the meeting without an agenda or clear focus, reading from his 50-slide PowerPoint presentation while other attendees feign listening while responding to texts and emails. When the project lead finishes and asks for questions, there is some heated debate on who owns the various processes involved in making the recommended changes. Most express their concern over whether or not the changes are actually necessary. Tom is among those who leave amid the debate to make it to his next meeting.

A few miles away, Sara's day begins by going to the coffee shop in her new office building. She orders her favorite drink, acknowledges several colleagues who are seated around her, grabs a table, turns on her computer, and plans out her day using a tool she received from a workshop her company recently hosted on increasing personal efficiency. Once she has her day planned, she checks her calendar and email. Today she is facilitating the design session in her team's weekly meeting. Sara always looks forward to her turn in leading this portion and feels energized to work with such talented and engaged professionals.

Novelty

On her way to the meeting, Sara passes a communication board with several opportunities to volunteer in the community or participate in focus groups. She decides to sign up for the "future of work" focus group. She recognizes several others who also have signed up, and she is excited to work with like-minded people and share her passion for and interest in how technology is changing the work environment.

In the hallway, a senior leader calls out her name and thanks her for her contribution to the quarterly report. Sara takes the opportunity to share with him her interest in learning more about the organization's lean initiative. He tells her to drop by his office sometime in the afternoon to pick up a resource he has found very helpful.

As Sara rounds the corner, she faintly hears upbeat music coming from the meeting room, which the team calls the "collaboration zone." She's impressed by her leader, who arrived a few minutes early to display a colorful, hand written agenda on the wall, arrange the tables to facilitate small groups, and place a wrapped package of Smarties candy at everyone's seat. She could never imagine a meeting looking like this at her previous company. Sara is the first to arrive and spends a few minutes brainstorming with her leader about the best way to handle a call she must make in the afternoon.

As team members arrive, they offer "high fives," the team's token handshake. The leader kicks off the meeting with a powerful but humorous story about the meeting's topic. Everyone agrees to the agenda, the ground rules, and the timeline. The leader reinforces one part of the company's mission statement that is particularly relevant to the task at hand. With applause, Sara enthusiastically takes the floor to lead the team in an interactive design session.

As she thanks everyone for their great work on last week's efforts, Sara wonders how Tom's day is going.

Overview

Novelty, innovation, and creativity are words spoken often, but their evidence is rarely seen. The stories of Tom and Sara are based on real workplaces where I have consulted. I remember going into Tom's Innovation Lab, which looked very impressive and convincing. However, although the company's marketing department and leadership frequently used the word "innovation" in speeches and glitzy publications, I never saw tangible examples. It was talked about but not lived out. I remember thinking, "If innovation appears here, I'm looking for unicorns in the parking lot."

Why? Because they had created a culture completely counter to innovation, creativity, and novelty.

This chapter is about the principle of Novelty, which I define as thinking bigger, differently, deeper, and forward. Novelty is about imagining larger than ever before, above and beyond what has been or what currently is. Novelty is about alternative thinking, a willingness to take action that veers from the expected and differs from conventional, accepted methods. Novelty is about diving deeper, strategically considering and analyzing motives, rewards, risks, and returns. And novelty is about looking ahead and taking a positive, solution-focused approach by viewing past decisions not as hindrances or failures but as valuable education that puts us in a better position for the future.

Cultures that don't embrace Novelty:

- "talk the talk" of novelty, innovation, and creativity;
- directly or indirectly punish risk-taking;
- have lost their sense of wonder, curiosity, and fun;
- do not reach beyond their industry for best practices;
- are late adopters;
- are characterized by high threat and low trust;
- have lots of bureaucracy that squelches interest and enthusiasm;
- have a "that-would-never-work-here" approach;
- avoid the tough talks that challenge its teams in positive ways; and
- implement initiatives to force collaboration rather than to build a culture where collaboration naturally occurs.

The consequences to such an environment impact not only individual lives but also the overall health and sustainability of the company. While the need to change and the requirement to adapt have always existed in the workplace, the speed of change in the workforce today (and in the future) is on overdrive. Novelty and the need for innovation and creativity are game-changers for who survives and who dies. I mean, have you rented a video from Blockbuster lately?

Cultures that embrace Novelty:

- "walk the walk" of novelty, innovation, and creativity;
- encourage risk-taking;
- honor and value input;
- honor and value differences;
- have a keen sense of wonder, curiosity, and fun;
- continuously and intentionally reach outside their industry for best practices;
- are early adopters;
- minimize bureaucracy;
- have work spaces conducive to collaboration;
- have a clear sense of purpose;
- adopt a "let's see how that could work here approach;"
- embrace and encourage the tough talks that challenge one another in positive ways;
- seek to continuously develop strengths, interests, and passions; and
- approach problems as challenges and opportunities for growth and change rather than threats and obstacles.

Often when I discuss the importance of novelty with leaders, I feel resistance. This is frequently accompanied by the "lean-back-in-the-chair-and-fold-arms" stance. One leader actually said, "This all sounds a little too touchy-feely. I have a business to run."

Let's see if embracing novelty in a culture is touchy-feely and happy-clappy, or if it makes good business sense. I mentioned Blockbuster, the movie rental company that failed to see a future in streaming movies and therefore rejected the opportunity to merge with Netflix. What about film and camera company Kodak, which failed to think bigger, differently, deeper, and forward as the digital age emerged? Or even television networks like CBS and NBC; they turned down the opportunity to host Monday Night Football, because who on Earth would be interested in watching football on television? And today's generations certainly aren't packing a Walkman, bag phone, or disposable camera to take on vacation.

Novelty has a bottom-line return. Just ask Amazon, Google, Zappos, Apple, Uber, Airbnb, and a host of other companies that have changed the game forever in their respective fields. The core of novelty is to be curious enough to ask "what if" and to be courageous enough to give it a try.

Reflection

- What comes to mind when you hear the word novelty?

- List three practices in your workplace you identify as novel?
- In your experience, what gets in the way of novelty?
- How would you rate the following in your workplace on a scale of 1-5, where 1 is "Strongly disagree" and 5 is "Strongly agree."

	1	2	3	4	5
We make time for fun.					
I can think differently from the group without repercussion.					
My ideas and opinions are valued.					
I am encouraged to take the time to think strategically.					
We are always looking ahead to "what's next."					
My organization is well positioned for the future.					
My organization questions and challenges the way things have been done in the past					
My organization values professional development					
My organization seeks to bring in new practices from different industries					
I can be creative and innovative at work					

Neurology & Science

There is a reason why companies that embrace novelty see an increase in retention, engagement, survivability, and profits; novelty is good for the brain. It wakes up the brain when just about everything in our world lulls our brains into a trance. Your brain doesn't pay attention to boring and it doesn't pay attention to familiar. How often do you drive on a route you take regularly but when you arrive, you can't remember anything about the trip? All you know is that you began the drive and ended up where you needed to be. But imagine if somewhere along the drive, something novel or unexpected had occurred; you would have immediately been jolted out of the "driver trance" or "highway hypnosis" we so frequently slip into behind the wheel. That's the power of novelty. It grabs us by the shirt collar and forces us to pay attention and remember.

We've all experienced the power of novelty thousands of times in our lives: that one presenter who stands out among the thousands of presentations we've sat through; that one professor, or one classroom moment, we remember even though we've endured thousands of hours of lecture; that one image we remember; that one stranger; that one moment on a vacation...and the list goes on. A novel event, whether a sign or a face or an experience, engages our brain, our emotions, and our memory system in a way that the routine, boring, and expected never will.

When I work with trainers and teachers to help them design learning that is aligned with how the brain learns best, I tell them to identify the most boring, expected part of their class or presentation. Then I ask them to focus on the part of their talk that even they dread. (I love the boring parts, because they provide the greatest opportunity to leverage the power of novelty.) I invite them to brainstorm 10 outrageous ideas or ways they can shake things up and do something drastically different and completely unexpected. This exercise can get interesting, to say the least.

The same technique works to turn dreaded, unproductive meetings into memorable ones that people actually look forward to. When I work with leaders and influencers who suffer from ineffective, unengaging, and unproductive meetings, we intentionally "flip" them simply by using the power of novelty. The return on incorporating novelty in classrooms and meeting rooms is better results and higher engagement.

One of my coaching clients, the facilitator for her HOA's monthly meetings, called one day out of pure apprehension and nausea. The meetings were tedious, unproductive, and a burden that caused her a great deal of anxiety. She literally had an adult beverage waiting at home for when the meeting ended; she even joked about wanting to sneak a flask into the gathering to help her get through the two hours of torture (and I am not convinced she was kidding about that...). In our discussion, we turned to the power of novelty, identified all the parts of the situation she dreaded, and became very creative and innovative.

She placed candies on the table and had generation-targeted music playing when the members arrived. She kicked the meeting off with a compelling story to unite the group and remind them of their importance. The story focused on a couple in the neighborhood, struggling with an illness, who were able to relocate and be near their family largely because of the property value of their home. She displayed a "scoreboard," which was a flipchart page labeled "Decisions." Each time a decision was made, a sticky note went up on the flipchart, and everyone did the "wave." She ended the meeting by showing a cartoon about HOAs. The members left laughing, feeling accomplished and valued, having much less dread of next month's meeting. And, my client reported needing less of her adult beverage when she went home that night.

Not only does novelty hold the power to capture the attention and shift the energy of an entire group, it also holds the secret to changing behavior. The Volkswagen auto company supported an initiative called "The Fun Theory," essentially an experiment to motivate people to change their behavior simply by making things fun. In one of my favorite videos from the campaign, the company wanted to see if they could encourage more people to choose taking the stairs over an escalator. The experiment involved converting a set of stairs at Stockholm's Odenplan subway station into working piano keys. The result of shifting the expected to the unexpected? Station-goers chose the stairs over the escalator 66% more than when the stairs were just...stairs. Conclusion: people tend to work harder when something is fun and interesting.

In other "The Fun Theory" experiments, people were more likely to use their seatbelts if the in-car entertainment system played only when the seatbelts were fastened. People were almost 100% more likely to recycle bottles using a bottle bank, when inserting the bottle mimicked a video game experience. And people were more likely to obey speed laws when the speed camera lottery was implemented; those who disobeyed the speed laws were caught by the camera, fined, and contributed to the lottery, while those who obeyed the laws were caught by the camera and were entered for a chance of winning the lottery.

As this exercise demonstrates, and as most of us have experienced in our own lives, novelty and fun are not only memorable and attention-grabbing, but they also change behavior—and the brain—for the better. The presence of novelty impacts the PFC, activates the brain's reward system, enhances memory and learning, promotes brain plasticity, and elevates important brain chemicals.

In previous chapters, I've mentioned the priceless functions of the PFC. This is the seat of abilities such as creativity and innovation, willpower, character, empathy, collaboration, and cooperation. If these are the outcomes we are looking for in our own lives and in the lives of those we influence, it is in our best interest to do everything possible to stimulate lots of activity in the PFC.

Negative threat dramatically deactivates this part of the brain. Of course, some level of anxiety or threat in the brain is a positive thing and can be motivational (i.e., I have a deadline to meet in writing this book, and I'd like to avoid the consequences). What is perceived as positive threat and negative threat can be different for each individual. But when any kind of negative threat (something we perceive as having a bad outcome and as being out of our control) is present, the PFC's functions are definitely compromised. The goal, then, is always to minimize threat so we don't shut down the functions of the PFC.

One of the reasons why novelty elicits such great results, grabs attention, and motivates people to change their behavior is because the right kind of novelty lowers negative threat. High negative threat and high fun usually don't exist in the same space. Much like a teeter-totter, as one increases, the other decreases. In a sense, novelty turns up the volume on the better part of who we are by turning down the volume of negative threat.

There are multiple examples of the benefits of introducing novelty even under the most stressful conditions. Physicians who see humor in everyday situations are less prone to depression and burnout, and they receive higher patient satisfaction ratings. Patients who use humor sleep better, remember more information told to them during their medical care, have reduced pain, and heal faster. Teachers who use novel approaches to learning in the classroom gain better engagement, improve test scores, and fewer behavior problems. Military personnel who were able to laugh reported reduced combat stress and improved cohesion of the group. Novelty lowers threat and increases prefrontal cortex activity.

In addition, novelty enhances brain function by impacting important chemicals in the brain. Exposure to surprise and a novel environment releases a rush of dopamine, a chemical in the brain important for heightened attention, focus, motivation, and goal-directed behaviors that activates the brain's reward system. When novelty triggers the brain to release dopamine, we are motivated to go explore in search of the reward.

I experienced this firsthand while on vacation in Mexico with my two adventurous, thrill-seeking teenagers. On our excursion, we were brought to a sinkhole and told we could jump in. That sounded fine until I looked down and realized the fall would be at least 50 feet. My son and daughter jumped without hesitation. I, on the other hand, summoned the power of novelty. Fear, too, showed up big-time, but not negative fear. The novelty of the moment activated dopamine which aroused my reward system and caused me to crave the reward of jumping, and I envisioned conquering my fear, free-falling and plunging into the beautiful water, being an "equal" to my teenagers, and bragging to my friends for the rest of my life. So, I took a deep breath and...jumped.

Novelty, of course, is short-lived. Things that were once novel can quickly become familiar. (Can you say "PowerPoint?") Much like the effects of a drug, novelty can leave the brain craving greater dopamine release to activate the reward system. It can propel us to seek more novelty. In the case of the sinkhole, after my kids jumped several times, they discovered there was a higher platform that would increase the drop by 10 more feet. In time, even the novelty of jumping from the higher platform became boring. I personally had to draw the line when they considered doing backflips into the sinkhole.

The reward center of the brain is located in the midbrain and is responsible for regulating reward as well as motivation. It seems to respond best to absolute novelty—completely new things or experiences—rather than relative novelty. The brain is a tough sell and not easily entertained for long. We seem to be hard-wired to seek out novelty, and when absolute novelty becomes relative novelty, we have a craving to search for more novelty.

The reward center is also closely linked to two areas of the brain critical to emotion, memory, and learning—the hippocampus and the amygdala. The hipopcampus sorts, files, and deletes information, especially when we sleep at night, to enhance memory and learning. This may be one reason why novelty is such a powerful teaching tool. In one study, the plasticity of the hippocampus (the ability to create new connections between neurons) was increased by the influence of novelty. Not only did the plasticity of the hippocampus increase during the process of exploring a novel environment or stimuli, the plasticity continued to increase for up to fifteen to thirty minutes after the novel exposure. Therefore, one effective learning and memory strategy is to set aside time to reflect and process information after taking in novel stimuli.

Novelty also activates the amygdala, an almond-shaped structure in the midbrain responsible for powerful emotions, especially fear. A great deal has been published on the amygdala largely because of its predicted role in PTSD. The amygdala has been referred to as the integrative center for emotions, emotional behavior, and motivation. It appears that the release of dopamine triggered by the novel stimuli actually reduces anxiety in the amygdala, activating rather than hijacking the prefrontal cortex, which enhances learning and memory.

Other important chemicals that novelty activates in the brain are serotonin, oxytocin, and endorphins. Serotonin, a chemical produced by nerve cells, fuels the brain, sparks curiosity, and impacts virtually every area of the body. Serotonin stabilizes mood, reduces depression, affects sleep and sexual function, and contributes significantly to overall health and happiness. Oxytocin, the hug hormone, facilitates bonding and triggers emotional responses that allow us to relax and trust. And finally, novelty elevates endorphins, the neurotransmitters that assist in blocking pain and experiencing pleasure and a sense of satisfaction.

Lastly, novelty impacts the brain's overall plasticity. Research has shown that a depressed brain can actually begin to shrink or atrophy. A happy brain, on the other hand, has greater neuroplasticity, the ability to heal and form new neural connections. When we have happy brains, we are more open to change, are more flexible and adaptable, have a greater ability to see situations from various perspectives, and can more easily synthesize new experiences and information with existing experiences and information. Good Think co-founder Shawn Achor, in his brilliant and popular TED talk, calls this the "Happiness Advantage"—more on that in the upcoming chapter on Using Emotion.

Application

A few years ago, Nissan had a series of commercials that were messaged with a powerful word...shift. The ads sold the concept of shifting...style, freedom, creativity, desire, evolution, exhilaration. Basically, they wanted viewers to see Nissan as novel and different, and I loved the idea. Like Nissan's message, most workplaces need to shift. If we want to unleash the power of novelty, it's a requirement that we shift beliefs and behaviors.

Innovation and creativity, the fruits of novelty, are desperately sought-out commodities in the workplace. Most organizations are in a whirlwind of change, and increasing competition, innovation, and creativity are essential to meet the demands of a rapidly changing, fiercely competitive world. The majority of companies where I consult want creativity and innovation, and they often incorporate those words into their mission, vision, and value statements. They are "talking the talk" but hesitant, or maybe ignorant, in how to "walk the walk."

If novelty, and therefore creativity and innovation, are ever to become a reality, we need to closely evaluate which actions need to shift. Our actions will either leverage or kill the power of novelty. We also need to shift behaviors that prevent or extinguish novelty. The behaviors that become acceptable in a culture will either wake up the brain and spark curiosity or threaten the brain and maintain the status quo. Finally, we need to challenge long-held beliefs. Ultimately, it's our beliefs that drive the results we experience. The reality is the choices in our daily actions, behaviors, and beliefs hold the power to hinder novelty or promote novelty.

It may be time we...shift.

Shift...from threat to trust

If I could share with the world the greatest leadership choice that can ever be made, I would share this: "Be proactive in minimizing threat." In all my years studying how the brain learns, the most powerful message we all need to hear is that threat kills, steals, and destroys. It kills our ability to perform at our best. It steals from individuals the ability to reach their full potential. And it destroys organizations, preventing them from the engagement, passion, ownership, and innovation that is essential to surviving in a highly competitive, fast-paced world that grows more and more complex and complicated every day.

Science has proven that negative threat, that which we perceive as harmful and over which we have little control, damages the brain. Among other consequences, threat increases cortisol, which makes us more prone to illness and disease; diminishes the priceless functions of the PFC; compromises our ability to learn and remember; and even causes parts of the brain to shrink or die. The brain is the equipment that drives retention, engagement, survivability, profits, and innovation. Why, then, are so many cultures characterized by toxic threat? The priceless returns we crave, especially that of innovation, simply cannot exist and grow in a high-threat environment.

While I'm remembering old commercials, another one that made me laugh promoted a well-known aerospace company. At the end of the commercial, a slogan slid across the bottom of the screen: "We are all about innovation."

My reaction was, "Really? Because do you know where innovation comes from? And have you truly crafted a culture where innovation can exist in the first place?"

I consulted for several years in one company, the one upon which Greg's story is based. They prided themselves on "embracing novelty and promoting innovation;" the very words even appeared in their mission and values statements.

In reality, the environment was inhospitable to both novelty and innovation, and the likelihood of that organization ever seeing innovation (which is a direct product of novelty) was, in my opinion, less than 1%. Why? They had built a culture of threat.

For those with a green thumb, you know certain kinds of plants, trees, and vegetables need certain kinds of environments in which to grow. The needs of an apple tree are different from the needs of a cactus. I don't have a green thumb; in fact, I don't even have one living plant in my house. But even I know that to produce fruit, you need the right environment.

This analogy is so relevant to the principle of novelty. To grow novelty, we need to create the optimal environment, one of high trust.

In a high-trust environment, people feel safe to explore, share, experiment, learn, fail temporarily, and grow. How someone does something matters as much as what they do. There is an intense focus on living out character as well as building competence. People and relationships are valued as much as bottom-line results and monetary returns. Leaders in high-trust organizations never lose sight of the fact that people are their most valuable resource. They know and live out the belief that their company is only as strong as its people.

One common denominator on Fortune's "100 Best Companies to Work For" list is trust. In companies such as Google and GoDaddy, employees trust management to keep them informed of important issues and changes with communication that is direct, transparent, and honest. Employees believe leadership is honest and ethical in their business practices, delivers on promises, and consistently "walks the talk." Their employees are flourishing as are their profits, largely because they shifted their actions, behaviors, and beliefs in their culture from high threat to high trust.

Shift...from weaknesses to strengths

While 'strengths' has gained ground over the last several years, our culture remains fixated on closing gaps. We test little Johnny at an early age to identify his weaknesses, often assigning him a diagnosis and adjusting our expectations of him accordingly. Throughout Johnny's childhood, we continue to attempt to close his gaps, testing him regularly to make sure they are still there. Johnny is likely to be exposed to that same deficit-focused mentality when he participates in sports, goes to church, and attempts to please his family and friends. When Johnny moves into his career, he faces the annual performance review when his manager will continue to help him see his ongoing gaps.

I'm not saying we should never work to improve where we are not strong. I'm not saying we should never give direct constructive criticism. I'm not saying everyone should get a trophy, and I definitely do not subscribe to the "if you had fun, you won" mentality. In reality, we all have weaknesses and areas where we need and absolutely must improve. But when the focus of a culture is, at any time in our lives, wholly focused on the things we suck at, aren't gifted to do, or were never designed to do, we kill the human spirit.

One poignant example of this is the fable, "The Animal School," written in 1940 (long before brain imaging) by George Reavis, superintendent of the Cincinnati Public Schools:

149

Unforgettable Leadership

Once upon a time the animals decided they must do something heroic to meet the problems of a "new world" so they organized a school. They had adopted an activity curriculum consisting of running, climbing, swimming and flying. To make it easier to administer the curriculum, all the animals took all the subjects. The duck was excellent in swimming. In fact, better than his instructor. But he made only passing grades in flying and was very poor in running. Since he was slow in running, he had to stay after school and also drop swimming in order to practice running. This was kept up until his webbed feet were badly worn and he was only average in swimming. But average was acceptable in school so nobody worried about that, except the duck. The rabbit started at the top of the class in running but had a nervous breakdown because of so much makeup work in swimming. The squirrel was excellent in climbing until he developed frustration in the flying class where his teacher made him start from the ground up instead of the treetop down. He also developed a "charlie horse" from overexertion and then got a C in climbing and D in running. The eagle was a problem child and was disciplined severely. In the climbing class, he beat all the others to the top of the tree but insisted on using his own way to get there. At the end of the year, an abnormal eel that could swim exceedingly well and also run, climb and fly a little had the highest average and was valedictorian. The prairie dogs stayed out of school and fought the tax levy because the administration would not add digging and burrowing to the curriculum. They apprenticed their children to a badger and later joined the groundhogs and gophers to start a successful private school.[1]

It seems so ridiculous to set up a school that punished students for obvious weaknesses at the expense of developing their obvious strengths. And yet, doesn't that look a lot like our current learning environments?

It seems ludicrous to put people in jobs that aren't the right fit, and then evaluate and compensate them on their performance of tasks they never had a propensity or

---

1   Reprinted with permission.

passion for in the first place. And yet, doesn't that look a lot like our current work environments?

If we want to reap the rewards of novelty, such as innovation, creativity, and peak performance, we must stop the trend of gap closing and shift to strengths finding. In "The Animal School," if the focus had shifted to strengths, the rabbit would have avoided a nervous breakdown and years of counseling that most likely ensued, and the duck may have gone on to establish an international school of swimming and mentor thousands of troubled ducklings.

Organizations that choose to identify and build on strengths get results. As mentioned earlier, a Gallup study found that organizations with leadership that focused on strengths enjoyed 73% engagement, as opposed to 9% engagement at those organizations whose leaders ignored strengths. Engaged employees are not only happy, they also are contributors who are loyal, more productive, quicker to learn new roles, and more creative and innovative. In addition, they cause fewer problems. Shifting from weaknesses to strengths is an inexpensive leadership tool that elicits an immeasurable impact to both the individual and the organization.

Shift..from confusion to clarity

Just like the brain has a craving for novelty, it also craves to know why. This is one of the first questions children ask: "Why, Mama? Why, Daddy?" And the hunger for the answer seems to haunt us from cradle to grave. We all crave purpose, meaning, and fulfillment, and wind up living much of our lives in pursuit of the why. Knowing the why—the bigger picture and the compelling vision—is not only the principle of relevance but is also critical to the principle of novelty. People are motivated and inspired to think bigger, deeper, forward, and differently when there is a clear, motivating purpose.

NASA has endless examples of how clear purpose and direction inspires novelty, creativity, and innovation. Apollo 13's mission was to land on the moon. When the mission was abruptly changed due to unexpected circumstances, and with time of the essence and the pressure of the whole world watching, the entire NASA team simply... shifted. Their mission changed. They were no longer going to the moon; they were bringing the astronauts home safely. Having this clear and compelling purpose spawned enormous novelty and innovation, including using duct tape and socks to build a filter. Another example from NASA, years later, was the mission to reduce the weight of rockets. With that clear purpose in mind, someone had the novel idea to test if the paint currently used on the tank was vital for protection. When it was discovered that it, in fact, wasn't, they stopped painting the tanks, freeing up another 600 pounds.

We often see the power of purpose in larger-than-life stories, such as that of Erik Weihenmayer, who climbed Mount Everest. More than 4,000 people have climbed the mountain, but what makes Weihenmayer's story a novelty is that he climbed Everest blind. Many variables united the climbing team, but by far the most powerful is that they were all clear on the mission: to get Weihenmayer to the top. The group encountered several challenges, not the least of which was guiding the blind American climber through the most treacherous terrain in the world where nearly 300 people have died. The heart and passion of this team is inspiring. Picked not only for competence but also for their character, team members were laser-focused on their purpose. Because there was no confusion on their mission, they collaboratively thought deeper, bigger, forward, and differently. The result? Nineteen of the 21 teammates reached the summit, the most climbers from a single team to reach the summit in a single day.

Shift...from silos to collaboration

Rarely does novelty happen in a silo. Granted, Chuck Noland, Tom Hanks' character in the film "Castaway," was pretty darn novelty-driven to survive being stranded on an uninhabited island for four years. But scenarios like that are anomalies; most of us are never going to be stranded on a deserted island, and novelty rarely happens when we are shut away from the world, working in isolation.

Most examples of novelty happen when we are collaborating with diverse groups of people possessing diverse skills, thought processes, perspectives, and approaches. Organizations, work teams, and individuals who see the greatest fruits novelty has to offer are those who value differences. The digital age has provided us with more tools for collaboration than we can really wrap our minds around. We are only limited by our own ability to think differently, deeper, bigger, and forward. Local and even global collaboration now happens at lightning speed.

We have outlets for nearly every kind of collaboration possible for nearly every size and purpose, and the tools and platforms to facilitate collaboration are prolific. Freelancers have access to multiple platforms to show their skills and find projects. Entrepreneurs can leverage the power of sites such as Etsy, Pinterest, Craigslist, and eBay. Small business owners can level up with powerhouses such as Amazon. We have crowdfunding platforms, shared workspaces, shared living spaces, and more social media outlets and groups than I could begin to list here.

One gift of collaboration is a novel outcome, one that is typically greater, more innovative, and more effective than what any person alone could have imagined. However, a second (and perhaps more powerful) gift of collaboration is ownership. When we help create the final product, and co-create the solution, we have a piece of ownership in it. Ownership simply means accountability, emotion, and engagement are built in, which lowers resistance and motivates us to support what we had a part in creating.

The barrier to collaboration is not a lack of tools and technology; rather, it is the human factor. Collaboration is an issue of trust, and to truly accomplish it, we must trust in each other and the process. Collaboration also is an issue of communication, requiring that we communicate with extreme clarity and in continuous, calculated ways. And finally, collaboration is an issue of unconditional positive regard. Genuine collaboration occurs when we wholly embrace and truly value the background, experiences, opinions, skills, culture, and perspectives of people who are different—sometimes drastically—from ourselves. Without a doubt, collaboration is an extremely sophisticated ability. If we want to harness the power of novelty, our actions, behaviors, and beliefs must shift from silos to collaboration.

Shift..from sick to healthy

American workers are growing...and I'm not talking about personal growth. The Centers for Disease Control and Prevention report that today's average American female weighs the same as the average male in the 1960's, and today's average American male weighs one and half times what the average female weighed back then. That's an 18.5% increase for women and a 17.6% increase for men. According to the study, 69% of adults over age 20 are either overweight or obese, as are nearly one-third of children between ages 10-17. Obesity increases the likelihood of heart disease, diabetes, strokes, and a host of other costly illnesses and life-limiting circumstances.

In addition to weight gain, Americans are growing in stress, overload, distraction, lack of sleep, and mental illness. Though Americans are using more of their vacation days than they did in previous years, they are still leaving more than 650 million days on the table, with women typically taking less days than men. In a 2014 Gallup poll, 40% of U.S. employees said they work more than 50 hours each week, while 20% exceeded 60 hours. American workers suffer from email and technology addiction. One study found American workers check their email a whopping 15 times per day, spending more than six hours total doing it. While the recommended amount of sleep for adults is 7-9 hours a night, 30% of American workers get less than 6 hours. That percentage of sleep deprivation increases to 40% for those working a night shift. And, while surfing the web for statistics on distraction, I found so many pop-up messages and ads that I got distracted and gave up. To top it all off, 50% of adults will develop a mental illness in their lifetime.

There is little "health" care in this country because today's overall focus seems to be on providing "sick" care. Our nation is sick, our workplaces are sick, and our schools and homes are sick. If we want to have healthy brains, we have to have healthy bodies. Healthy bodies and brains are essential to a healthy life and a healthy workplace. This concept is not a difficult one, and I have often thought of writing a book entitled, "Duh," until I discovered someone had beat me to it. Duh.

Novelty comes from a healthy brain via a healthy body and a healthy lifestyle. If an organization wants healthy people walking through their doors every day, they must have a health and wellness plan. There are numerous workplace health and wellness plans, including one provided by the CDC. The characteristics of a healthy workplace plan are multidimensional, beginning with a baseline assessment and supported by a number of solutions, ranging from healthy eating options in vending machines and the cafeteria, to gym memberships, to financial incentives for participating in health screenings and weight loss initiatives.

Any change, however, brings some level of threat. Though health and wellness programs in the workplace exist for the greater good of the individual and the company, leaders choosing to enact these must be prepared for likely resistance and upheaval. Previously, I discussed how I once consulted with a health insurance company that realized they were the unhealthiest company they insured. In response, one of their initiatives within their health and wellness plan was to forbid smoking anywhere on company property. They also revised their daily practice of having complimentary chips and sodas available to their employees and removed all unhealthy snacks from their vending machines. Health screenings became a requirement for continued employment, and the company offered financial incentives for participation in various health-enhancement programs.

As you can imagine, the changes were not instantly embraced by some. Employees resisted, complained, and even snuck in sodas and candy contraband. But the company stayed the course, and, in time, it shifted from the sickest organization they insured to one of the healthiest.

Shift...from despair to hope

Clearly, healthcare is one industry experiencing rapid change. In recent years, legislative changes have dramatically altered how healthcare is practiced and funded in this country, leaving healthcare providers, business owners, and individuals confused, scared, and scrambling to determine how to adjust accordingly. I attended a packed town hall led by local healthcare leaders with the focus of sharing ideas and strategies. One leader after another took the stage, stood at the podium before a packed crowd eager for answers, and delivered a message of "we will just have to wait and see what Washington does."

Except for one.

When this leader's turn came, he adjusted the mic and emphatically stated, "I represent XYZ health system, and we aren't waiting on Washington." The crowd literally broke out in applause. He proceeded to lay out a plan of how the system would continue and adjust, of how these adjustments would likely impact and benefit local business owners and individuals, and how others could get involved. He operated with the same unknowns as every other healthcare leader in the room that night. The difference was that he shifted his focus from despair to hope, from a problem-focus to a solution-focus.

Unforgettable Leadership

Early in my career I personally experienced the power of this approach. I worked for a defense company that was being purchased by a global organization, and restructuring and layoffs were inevitable. The rumors were flying, and people were scrambling to update resumes and rebuild long-neglected networks. Our leader called our team together, as we were clearly on the chopping block. She directly addressed the grim reality of the situation then proceeded to share her inspiring vision for our team: "We are here, and we need to get there. What do we need to do?" Enthusiastically, the team collaborated and determined novel ways and ideas to get us to the vision. In the end, not one member of our team was cut, and through the purchase, our leader managed to position our services as vital to the company's new direction.

As a coach, I've witnessed the power of shifting from despair to hope so many times. People seek coaches for a variety of reasons, but often it is because they are sick and tired of being sick and tired. A few seek coaching when they are in despair; others seek coaching because they are excelling and desire more. Either way, some level of struggle or discomfort usually surfaces in the coaching process. Change simply requires it. One role of a coach is to keep the client moving toward a compelling vision. I often say, "It's OK to circle the drain. We just can't stay there." When a coach is able to shift the focus to hope and lead the client to think forward, an unlimited number of creative and innovative options suddenly become available.

Novelty

An excellent example of this shift involved a client, "Lisa." She was a director who sought coaching to help her reach her goal of moving into a VP position that would soon be open. Only a few weeks into our sessions, she learned her counterpart was offered the position. Despair ensued. But by encouraging her to shift to hope, to shift from problem to solution, she dreamed of and detailed her ideal work culture. This shift allowed her to think far beyond a VP position. Today, she is a CEO.

The brain on despair is quite different than the brain on hope, and the brain on problems is not as functional as the brain on solutions. When we can clearly define, feel, and visualize where we are going versus where we are, the brain is flooded with novel solutions. For every problem, there really are multiple solutions. By shifting our actions, behaviors, and beliefs from despair to hope, we unleash the novel potential.

The brain is the equipment that drives retention, engagement, survivability, profits, and every other dream and result that gets us up and out of bed every morning. Novelty is one way to supercharge the brain, the most important piece of equipment on the planet. When our actions are overseen by our best brain, we definitely produce our best work. But even greater, we live our best lives.

A glimpse into the lives of Tom and Sara at the start of this chapter—real lives in real cultures where I have consulted—reveals two highly committed, bright professionals investing a great deal of themselves in their jobs at their workplaces.

Every day, Tom walks into an environment where novelty simply cannot survive. He struggles to function in a culture that pays lip service to novelty but shows very little evidence that it is a deeply held value. In his world, novelty ends with impressive letters in wall signs and glitzy marketing publications. He is trapped in a culture loaded with bureaucracy because of a need for ego and a lack of trust. Team members have very little sense of value and belonging and resort to existing in silos rather than striving for collaboration. No one is clear on how what they do contributes to the whole.

Sara, on the other hand, enters each day into an environment in which novelty can't help but exist. Novelty, creativity, and innovation thrive there because people feel valued, welcomed, and appreciated. They have a clear direction and clear alignment with how each job moves the proverbial needle. There is high trust among the team and with leadership, and there is a true sense of camaraderie. Multiple opportunities to grow personally and professionally and to contribute to important causes exist within her organization.

So, of the two, which person is most likely to produce the best work and live the best life? My bet is on Sara.

Charles Darwin is noted to have said, "It is not the strongest or the most intelligent who will survive but those who can best manage change." Along that same line, the companies and schools that will survive and win will not necessarily be the ones with the most funding or the best technology; they will be those that change and adapt faster than the competition.

Foundational to adapting and embracing change at the speed of sound is creating an environment where novelty can thrive.

An inspiring purpose, shared by the entire group, gives life to novelty. As the old saying goes, "Necessity is the mother of invention." If we seek novel solutions to problems, let's define a vision and provide a necessity—a purpose—that people are compelled to be a part of.

Interaction

| Empowering through choice and voice

Tell them, they comply.
Involve them, they commit.

I can't stay here anymore. I've made a huge mistake." This is how Natalie began her Thursday morning session with her coach.

Natalie was a confident research manager at a nationally ranked medical institute. But wanting to grow her career and expand her development, she assumed a director role at another healthcare system. This bold move required relocating to another part of the country, taking on more research responsibility, overseeing approximately 80 employees, and moving way beyond her comfort zone. Thus, she hired a professional coach to help her successfully move through the transition.

Interaction

Thirty days into her new role, she sat, defeated, on the phone with her coach, questioning every decision she had made. The challenge was more than she imagined when she accepted the position. Granted, she knew the teams she inherited were the result of three separate mergers, so she expected some territorialism. Yes, she was aware there were some performance problems she would need to address, so she expected to have a few tough conversations. What she didn't expect were those challenges...on steroids!

Natalie's coach responded to her dramatic opening words calmly with, "Tell me more about what's going on."

Natalie took a deep breath, sighed, then explained that the three teams she supervised refused to interact with anyone except their legacy teammates. In fact, the three teams physically sat in three separate sections of the room. Team members missed work without calling, showed up late without notifying her or giving any explanation, and refused to complete assignments. Her days were spent solving problems the team encountered or mediating conflict between team members. She was not sleeping at night and battling terrible headaches. But the worst consequence by far for Natalie was that she felt like a complete failure.

Natalie's coach asked her, "Out of these challenges, which would you like to focus on?"

Natalie thought for a moment. "I'm just tired of feeling like a parent of rebellious children. I feel like all I do every day is solve everybody's petty problems."

Her coach asked, "What is the impact when you assume the role of parent/problem-solver?"

Natalie immediately responded, "I'm exhausted and angry. I feel resentful toward my team because it keeps me from doing the thing that I love—leading research."

Then her coach asked, "What is the impact on your team when you assume the role of parent/problem-solver?"

"They just do more of the same," Natalie responded. "They keep expecting me to solve more problems. I had one research manager come into my office three times yesterday with either a personnel problem or a research problem."

After a pause, Natalie's coach asked, "So I've heard you say you are exhausted, feeling like the parent and the problem-solver. Is that correct?"

"That's exactly right."

Her coach then challenged her: "Think about the research manager you mentioned. What other approaches besides parent/problem-solver could you have taken?"

Natalie said, "Well, I could have told her to go talk to the problem team member herself, so I wouldn't have had to."

"Yes, what else?"

Natalie continued, "I could have told her to find a mentor in the company who had handled a similar situation."

Her coach encouraged, "Yes, what else?"

Natalie reflected before answering. "I guess I could have just asked the manager what she recommended."

"Yes," her coach replied. "Out of those different approaches, what seems best to you now?"

Natalie laughed. "The best option now is for me to turn the problem over to its owner. After all, she is a seasoned manager. She's really experienced, and the team seems to respect her."

Natalie's coach asked, "What benefits would that approach have over the parent/problem-solver approach?"

Natalie responded, "It would definitely develop and grow her. She would have ownership and accountability. And it would let her know that I believe in her and that I value her. Now that I think about it, I think that approach would work for several of the problems I'm encountering. Instead of assuming I need to run around and fix and solve everything, I could assume they are quite capable of solving their own problems and just provide the support they need."

Her coach asked, "What would open up for you if you shifted from solving problems to asking questions?"

Natalie sighed with relief. "I would definitely sleep better. I believe my headaches would go away. I could get back to doing the things I love and what drew me to the job in the first place. And I really think the team would respect me more. Now that I think about the situation clearer, maybe my team is actually resenting me for solving problems for them. I think I have communicated to them subconsciously that I don't trust them or think they are capable."

Natalie's coach pressed ahead. "I have two more questions, okay?"

"Sure."

"Based on what we've discussed, what are your next steps?"

Natalie responded, "The next time someone comes to me with a problem, I'm going to pause. I'm going to fight the urge to rush in and solve it for them. Instead, I'm going to place the problem back in their lap, ask questions to help them discover the best solution, and then provide whatever support they feel they need."

"And my final question," the coach offered. "How does that feel? I know you were really burdened and frustrated when we began the call. How would you describe how you're feeling now?"

Natalie responded with a smile. "I feel excited, actually, like a weight has been lifted off my shoulders."

Overview

One of those most difficult shifts to make is to shift from tell to involve. This struggle shows up in all areas of education, from the peer tutor working with a college learner, to the K-12 classroom teacher with a full room of students, to the workplace trainer facilitating a workshop, to parents attempting to expand their child's thinking, to the leader desiring to develop employees and lead the organization. For 99% of the population, telling and solving is the default. For a multitude of reasons, asking and involving seems counter-intuitive, unpredictable, awkward and uncomfortable. It must be deeply hard-wired in our DNA that we have developed the desire to solve problems and give information rather than lead others to discover the information or solve their problems for themselves.

This chapter focuses on the principle of Interaction. Interaction is what we see when people are not only given a choice and a voice, but also are expected to exercise their choice and voice. Choice and voice are highly valued commodities. The Interaction principle is at work when learners are fully engaged in the educational process, when teams are wholeheartedly collaborating, and when people participate in meaningful conversations and sincerely work together to discover the optimal solution.

You will discover in this chapter that cultures that adopt the principle of Interaction see sustainable returns, while those that do not pay a dear price. Mainly, they stay stuck. They create uncessary problems for themselves. They will be left behind.

In cultures operating without Interaction:

- The length of training sessions is determined by the number of slides the instructor will read.
- Training becomes a "check-the-box" experience rather than a transformational one.
- Leaders spend the majority of their time "putting out fires" and solving everyone's problems.

- Leaders find their worth and feed their egos by "putting out fires" and solving everyone's problems.
- HR becomes the organizational babysitter, dealing with petty, unnecessary people-problems.
- Employees have the option to "check their brains in at the door."
- Employees learn quickly that their thoughts, experiences, and opinions aren't really welcomed.
- Team members spend countless hours reliving injustices from the past and confessing the sins of others.
- Productivity comes to a halt until someone with the proper authority makes a decision or attempts to identify the root cause of the problem.
- Individual conflict builds until it reaches the point where someone "tattles in the principal's office," or worse, brings the case to court.
- Blaming, finger-pointing, criticizing, and condemning characterize the culture more accurately than ownership and accountability.
- Leaders hold two beliefs: they have the right answer, and others want to be told their right answers.
- Leaders operate under the false assumption that results are more predictable, controllable, and sustainable when people are given the solutions rather than discovering them for themselves.
- Learned helplessness, a condition describing someone who suffers from a profound sense of

powerlessness, translates into apathy, paralysis, and attrition.

I remember a scene from the animated movie, "A Bug's Life," that captures this kind of culture. It's the opening scene when the ants are doing what they do every day: gathering food and mindlessly getting into a single-file line to where they are expected to drop off the food. The scene always makes me laugh, because I can see all of us getting out of bed, completing our morning routines, then sitting in a line of cars during rush-hour traffic. The two scenes are dangerously similar.

As the ants are carrying out their normal routine, a large leaf appears out of nowhere and falls in front of one of the ants, blocking the path and causing a moderate pile-up in the single-file line. The ants are terrified. The first ant to encounter the leaf pauses and nervously screams in sheer panic that he is lost.

In the crisis moment, a "boss" ant comes to the rescue. With a calm, confident voice, he marches down the hill to the distraught line, all the while encouraging the work ants not to panic because they have everything under control. He proclaims that he is a trained professional. In other words, we have more knowledge than you do, and we are going to solve this problem for you.

The "boss" ant looks directly into the eyes of the ant leading the confused line. He takes charge, physically guides the ant, and gives the directive to go around the leaf. The worker ant protests and questions whether or not they are allowed to do that. When the ant relents and cautiously starts to walk around the leaf, the "boss" ant claps his hands and offers words of encouragement.

See the similarities? The leaf is not a great deal different from a process that breaks, leaving people spinning and unable to make a decision or solve the problem. The conflict rattles the team, crippling their performance and ability to move forward amid uncertainty. Their "gravy client" may be lost. That big order might be cancelled. The project plan really isn't so...planned. A key person announces she is leaving the company. Any of these can leave people in an organization nervously saying, "Oh no, what do I do?" And then scream, "I'M LOST!"

Some people want to be rescued, to have a superhero rush in to save the day. Often, leaders crave that role. They want to march in with confidence and swagger, allay all fears, and wisely give the next steps. The problem is, while the team may "go around the leaf" and resume marching in line, what happens when the next leaf falls? And the leaf after that? And what if the leader is not around (at lunch, or, heaven forbid, on vacation) when the leaf falls?

Cultures that embrace the principle of Interaction are less about solving and telling, and more about involving and developing.

In cultures operating with Interaction:

- A training session will be highly interactive and engaging.

- The length and delivery method of the training session will be defined by the needs of the learner—not the organization.
- The intended outcome of all learning experiences is not to check a box but to transform thinking, performance, and behavior.
- Leaders spend the majority of their time helping others think through their challenges and how to solve them.
- Leaders find their worth and contribute to the overall growth of the team by helping others identify the best possible solutions and strategies for putting those solutions into action.
- HR becomes a resource center, providing growth and development opportunities to help leaders and individuals achieve their goals.
- Employees grow, develop, and advance based on how they add value to the organization through sharing their thoughts, experiences, and opinions.
- Team members hold each other accountable and redirect conversations to find solutions rather than stay stuck in problems.
- Members at all levels of the organization are empowered and expected to take action.
- Individual conflict presents an opportunity for growth.
- Taking ownership, holding self and others accountable, and following through characterizes

the culture more accurately than blaming, finger-pointing, criticizing, and condemning.

- Leaders hold two beliefs: there is not one right answer, and better solutions happen when all parties identify the answer together.
- Results are more predictable, controllable, and sustainable when people explore the problem, identify possible solutions, and choose solutions that work best.
- Learned helplessness, a condition describing someone who suffers from a profound sense of powerlessness, is not expected, rewarded, or even tolerated.

We often think it's faster or it's cheaper to tell and solve. After all, who has time to ask all these questions? Many people believe they have the one right answer, and it is their job to tell the world what that is.

Problem is, that approach is only faster and cheaper in the short-term. For those of us who have made the shift, we know the "tell and solve" approach is neither faster nor cheaper because compliance is short-lived. We are aware that a different approach is needed if we want to have sustainable returns, those that happen when we grow and develop ourselves, others, and relationships.

To do that, we must leverage the Interaction principle. We meet people where they are, without judgment, and with a mindset of "power with" rather than "power over." We co-discover or co-create solutions. When we meet people in this way, we find solutions that we had not previously considered or create solutions that had not previously existed. But the solution itself is not the real return. The real return of interaction is the development, ownership, accountability, and loyalty that result from being involved in the process.

It is true: tell people, and they will comply, but involve them, and they will commit. Like you, I'm interested in genuine commitment.

Reflection

- Write down two or three words you would associate with the following roles:
  - Boss
  - Mentor
  - Coach
- What image comes to mind when you think of a coach?
- Consider how would you respond to the following scenario:

  A co-worker walks into your office and shuts the door. She says she is so frustrated with someone who is a peer to you both. She says, "I can't work with him anymore. He's driving me crazy!"

- In your experience, what does it mean to be coachable?

- List two or three positive experiences or people that have helped you become who you are today?
- Take a moment to rate the degree to which you either agree or disagree with the following beliefs on a scale of one to five, where one is strongly disagree, and five is strongly agree:

	1	2	3	4	5
Better solutions result when we come to a conversation in a state of not knowing.					
People respond to their view of reality and not necessarily to reality itself.					
The more choices we have in solving a problem, the more control and ownership we feel about the problem.					
Most people are best motivated by a positive, compelling vision.					
People already have the resources they need.					
The presenting problem is usually not the real problem.					
There is a reward for every choice, behavior, and action we take.					
Telling people results in compliance, but involving people results in commitment.					
The brain pushes back when told what to do.					

Neurology & Science

One of the best set of questions I have asked myself through the years and as I prepared to write this book began with "what if?" My first question was, "What if we really designed learning according to the principles of how the brain learns best?" After all, the brain must be in the forefront when designing learning; it's the seat of where learning occurs! If we don't, we've defeated our purpose and wasted a lot of time.

My second question was, "What if we really led ourselves, others, and organizations according to the principles of how the brain learns best?" Once again, the brain must be the prime consideration when we communicate and interact with others; it is the seat of where communication and transformation occur! Again, if we don't consider the impact on the brain, and why something either does or does not align with it, we are spinning our wheels and casting aside our valuable time and resources.

Interaction is no different from the other principles presented in this book. The reason why it is effective, and the reason why this principle helps leaders achieve impressive results with less effort, is because it aligns with how the brain works best. This is the magic formula! If we simply work with the way the equipment works, we will have fewer problems and achieve better results in an easier way.

Four areas of brain research support the principle of Interaction. The first is in the likelihood of learning and remembering information; if we want to increase the retention of information, we need to incorporate the principle of Interaction. The second area is in behavior change; if we want to lead change with less stress and resistance, we must integrate interaction. The third is in reducing threat; if we want to minimize the debilitating impact of threat and maximize the priceless functions of the prefrontal cortex, interaction is key. Fourth is learned helplessness; if we want to involve, empower, and utilize our most precious resources—our people resources—we must focus on interaction.

Retention

Training is a multi-billion-dollar industry. Regardless of the delivery method of training (traditional classroom, virtual, web-based, eLearning, one-on-one) or the content of training (leadership, job-specific), two things remain the same: the goal is to improve performance, and the equipment involved is the brain.

For centuries, educators have searched for the secrets to making learning easier and making it stick. One of the common denominators to all those successful secrets is the principle of Interaction.

Socrates and his philosophy students are famous for the Socratic method of questioning. As far back as 400 B.C., Socrates discovered the power in asking versus telling. In fact, he believed asking questions of oneself and others was the highest form of human excellence. He leveraged the powerful tools of asking deliberate, disciplined questioning to elicit feedback, probe understanding, and explore ideas.

While this method can still be effective today, it is often not used in a way that increases trust and decreases threat for the sake of deeper learning. Rather, lecturers often use the Socratic method as a method of interrogation and imposing threat rather than truly staying in a place of seeking feedback, understanding, and exploration.

Bloom's taxonomy is another structure for learning that relies on the principle of Interaction. In 1956, educational psychologist Edward J. Boom created a taxonomy to promote higher levels of retention, processing, and thinking. Essentially, the taxonomy is built on the premise that the more we engage in the process of learning, the more we move from a basic level of knowledge to more sophisticated levels of analysis, synthesis, and evaluation. Engagement or interaction, then, results in deeper levels of thinking and ownership.

For example, let's say I want someone to learn the eight steps for leading change explained in John Kotter's *The Heart of Change*. At the knowledge level, we could have our student list the eight steps. At the understanding level, we could have him reteach the eight steps and provide examples. But if we really want the learner to "own" the information, let's ask him to implement the eight steps as he actually leads a real organization through change, reflecting on what went well, the impact, what did not go well, and the cost. Then we would be at the higher levels of Bloom's taxonomy. Chances are this learner now has what I call a "deep-down-in-your-bones" kind of knowing.

Why? Greater engagement and interaction.

In recent years, organizations have explored what increases the likelihood of remembering information in an attempt to see a better return on the investment of their training dollars. Their findings are quite similar to what we've known for a long time; the greater the interaction, the greater the retention.

This research is especially memorable for me. I was part of a design group many years ago that spent hours designing a leadership program for a government agency. The content was robust, and the activities were highly interactive and engaging. We had a combination of multiple ways of learning including classroom, small-group projects, on-the-job applications, and so forth. We were more than pleased with our program, but when we presented the design, the client told us that we missed the mark. He wanted 40 hours of lecture (gasp!).

Clearly, learning and retention are complicated. Every brain is as unique as its owner's fingerprint and is always-changing. For that reason, I try to avoid neatly compartmentalized graphics giving nicely rounded percentages of retention. For example, if you've been in the world of education, you most likely have heard at some point statistics such as we only remember 10% of what we read, 20% of what we hear, and so forth. While there may not be scientific research to support these statistics, there is enough anecdotal evidence to support that "on average" we can increase retention by increasing interaction.

Common sense alone tells us that if we truly engage with something, we are more likely, on average, to remember it than if we were to just hear it.

An example in two scenarios: think about the last time you heard a joke you thought was funny. Chances are you laughed and wanted to remember the joke so you could tell it someone else. And chances are you forgot the joke within 24 hours. We've all been there.

But, what if, when you heard the joke, you wrote the joke down in your own words or drew an image of it, then retold the joke to 24 different people. Chances are very high that you would still remember the joke later on, even a few months from now. The difference between the two situations? The joke stayed the same, but in the second scenario, you interacted with the joke and made it yours. Now, you own the joke.

In the training world, we often talk about the 70/20/10 model, developed by experts at the Center for Creative Leadership. When developers Moran McCall, Michael M. Lombardo, and Robert W. Eichinger surveyed nearly 200 executives who self-reported how they believed they learned, the team discovered that roughly 70% of the executives surveyed learned from challenging assignments, 20% learned from meaningful relationships, and only 10% learned through formal courses or training.

Like with the nicely rounded percentages discussed earlier, let's avoid getting caught up in exact numbers. Some training organizations have taken these findings literally and revamped their training so that everything broke down into 70% assignments, 20% relationships, and 10% coursework. I don't think that's the point; what we need to focus on is that learning and development require interaction that is safe and meaningful.

Eric Jensen, the brain-based learning expert, tells us that the type of feedback we get when we are interacting with material and the length of time we interact with the material can also be influential. Jensen says we don't learn as fast with only positive feedback. While we are interacting with material, it is important that we receive corrective feedback that is specific rather than general.

As far as a time investment, Jensen says learning takes a lot longer than most of us think, and the worst predictors of how long something takes to learn are generally the subject-matter experts themselves. In fact, Jensen urges that the first introduction to something should be considered the rough draft. Most learning—unless there is a serious emotional charge—is never a "one-and-done." Too much information, given too quickly and without interaction, equals learning that doesn't last. Studies focused on the rigor of musicians, athletes, and chess players have revealed that to truly master something, we may need to engage and interact with it for as many as 10,000 hours or more. Though, again, every brain is unique and multiple variables impact how quickly we learn.

When it comes to truly learning and retaining information, there seems to be no replacement for interaction, time, and feedback. Jensen often talks about the 51-49 rule, an input-to-output ratio that is a tremendously helpful guideline when we engage with others and want them to interact. We should be talking 51% of the time, and they should be talking 49% of the time. Again, no magic in the exact numbers. The point is if you are talking, they are most likely not learning.

I often record calls with coaching clients, and one of the tools I use sends me a follow-up report listing the percentage of time each person talked. I challenge you to track the time you spend talking.

Changing behavior

Most often, both formal and informal training seek to change behavior. Everyone reading this book who leads change, who seeks to change themselves, or who strives to change others knows that this is a monumental task!

Why? Because it's hard.

Why is change so difficult, and what can we do to make it less difficult? Not to oversimplify, but change is hard because the brain resists it. The brain wants everything to stay the same, even if that new something is better for us.

What do we know, then, about how to increase the likelihood of changing behavior, especially when it comes to sustainable behavior change? We can learn a few lessons from programs that have been successful in helping people change their behavior for an extended time, programs such as Weight Watchers. A 2013 study by Weight Watchers found that more people lost weight with Weight Watchers (an average of 10.1 pounds at six months) than a self-help group (an average of only 1.3 pounds in the same time period.) The study then turned to who was most successful in the Weight Watchers group. It concluded that a client's level of interaction with the program had a correlation to the amount of weight lost. Those who had a high degree of interaction, attending 50 percent of the meetings and using the website and mobile app twice a week, lost an average of 19 pounds.

Other change programs, such as Alcoholics Anonymous, show comparable results. The greater the interaction with the program and community, the greater the likelihood of change and sustainable change.

Similar findings by Linda and Richard Eyre, authors of *Teaching Your Children Responsibility*, led them to determine the average success rate of changing behavior. In their study, they estimated a 16% likelihood of changing behavior if you hear an idea you like. The last time I heard of someone eliminating carbs from her diet, for example, I liked the idea; unfortunately, my success rate was not very high.

The Eyre's, however, found that successful behavior change rises to about 90% if we hear an idea we like, consciously decide to adopt it, decide when and how we will do it, and have a specific appointment with someone to report whether we have actually done it. (Confession. I didn't reveal that I removed carbs from my diet to anyone.)

Interaction also provides clarity, a critical variable in changing behavior. Most often, people are not resisting change so much as they are resisting confusion. When we interact, we can decrease confusion and increase clarity.

All successful behavior change involves willingness, accountability, and a great deal of interaction. Willingness is that it is a compelling idea to begin with. Accountability holds us to a measurable goal. Interaction means that we engage over time to foster ownership and provide clarity.

Threat

The brain pushes back when told what to do, and this is true at any age. For that reason, when we engage people through interaction, we don't interrogate them; we engage with them in a meaningful conversation. We seek and value their opinions, ideas, and insight. We stay interested and curious. As a result, we lower threat in the brain.

When people are participants in discovering a solution to a problem, the brain responds with "challenge" rather than "threat." Instead of being told what to do, causing the brain to push back, or frozen in the unknown, causing the brain to shut down, the principle of Interaction encourages others to be curious and discover the best solution, causing the brain to "come alive."

If you recall, threat elevates stress hormone levels, accelerating emotions and debilitating the prefrontal cortex, the seat of all those higher-order thinking and communicating abilities. When we "tell," and especially when we "demand," we turn down the PFC and turn up threat. However, when we involve, value, empower, and seek interaction, we turn on the prefrontal cortex and the "good" chemicals that accompany an active PFC, such as dopamine, serotonin, and norepinephrine.

Learned helplessness

Learned helplessness is a term coined by Martin Seligman, often referred to as "the father of positive psychology," to describe what happens in severe situations where people have lost the hope of having any chance of escape from their stress and/or pain. It can result in severe depression and dramatic brain decline. While all of us have heard the cruel stories of this condition impacting people in unthinkable situations, such as those in concentration camps or those held against their will in other types of deplorable experiences, learned helplessness can also affect people living in first-world countries if they fall victim to a toxic learning or work situation.

Dr. John Medina, in his book, *Brain Rules*, reveals that learned helplessness can trigger stress damaging enough to not only interfere with memory and learning but also our natural defense systems. Elevated stress hormones that can be caused by learned helplessness can literally shut down our natural defenses, particularly when exposed to prolonged or extreme stress.

Interaction is the opposite of learned helplessness. When leaders follow the principle of Interaction, they have "power with" rather than "power over" those they lead. Interaction requires staying curious, asking questions, involving others, valuing ideas, and welcoming input. Interaction empowers by giving others a choice and a voice.

Application

The power of the interaction principle truly comes to life when we assume the role of coach.

There are a few words we often use interchangeably when, in fact, they have very different meanings; three of those are boss, mentor, and coach. Earlier, I asked you to think about words you might use to describe boss, mentor, and coach. While all three of these roles are necessary, each has a unique meaning and impact on the culture and operate off distinct beliefs.

A closer look at their definitions leads to the origin of each word. The way you describe "boss" will most likely depend on your personal experience. If you once had a great boss, you might use a positive word like "leader." However, the origin of the word is actually "lord" or "master." This more closely resembles my personal experience; when I think "boss," I imagine someone "large and in charge," giving orders with a pointing finger. "Mentor" actually originates from Homer's epic poem, "The Odyssey." In the story, Athena transforms into a character named Mentor and guides Telemachus on his journey. She is the older, wiser, sage figure guiding and advising the less-experienced student along the path.

The origin of coach comes from the word "stagecoach." Initially, I was surprised when I discovered its meaning, but then I realized what a perfect image it is. The process of using a stagecoach is similar to the modern-day taxi, Uber, or Lyft. The coach meets you where you are and takes you to where YOU want to be; it's not the driver's job to tell you where to go. Primarily, the coach just gets you there safely and in the fastest way possible.

Certainly, if you aren't completely clear on your destination, he or she can give suggestions or help you figure out exactly what you're looking for. For example, while in Boston for a work event, I wanted to find a good place for dinner. I relied on the recommendation of the cab driver because I knew he was more familiar with the area, but ultimately, I was the one who set the direction. The same holds true in coaching. The coachee, and not the coach, is in charge of the final destination. The coach operates on the coachee's agenda.

All three roles—the boss, the mentor, and the coach— have value in the workplace, depending on the situation, but you must be aware of their differences. Boss, mentor, and coach operate off very distinctive beliefs. Let's take a look at why the beliefs underlying these roles are so critical.

One of the models I use in my coaching practice leads clients to see how their reality is connected by four important components (that are, by the way, within their control).

Here's a simple example of how the model works.

The four components are:
- My Reality (results and outcomes I want to change) is driven by
- My Actions (choices and behaviors I am taking) which are driven by
- My Feelings (what I am feeling) which are driven by
- My Beliefs (Thoughts and stories I have about my experiences) which are shaped by
- My Past Experiences (Experiences that create/reinforce my belief):

Let me illustrate:

If My Reality is that I have gained unwanted weight, this is happening because of My Actions. Let's say the actions leading to the reality are that I'm eating ice cream every night before bed. My Feelings are very often driving these actions. In this example, perhaps I am feeling overwhelmed and want to escape my stress.

My Beliefs are driving all of the above. Maybe the belief I have adopted is that I do not have control over my stress and that the only way to manage stress is through food. The only way, then, to truly shift the belief, which will then shift my feelings, actions, and results, is to have a new experience. The new experience in the weight gain example might be to handle my stress through ways other than food.

Oftentimes, to see change in reality, we have to reestablish the connection among these four components.

Out of the four components, beliefs is the most powerful. When we change our beliefs, we can more easily change our feelings, actions, and results. The question to ask, then, is "what belief is driving that feeling, action, choice, or behavior?"

This is especially true when it comes to leading as a boss, a mentor, or a coach. What beliefs underly each role?

If people act in the role of "boss," the role of "lord and master" over others, they most likely are driven by the belief that there is one right answer and they have it; that they have more knowledge than the people under them; that they have the right and responsibility to set the direction, and that others are obligated to obey without question.

All of us have seen this role in action in one way or another; does the phrase, "Because I said so" ring a bell? This gives us a feeling of superiority and authority. Then, we take actions like micromanaging, telling, and directing. Certainly, this is not always bad. However, we must be aware of how those beliefs and actions impact our reality.

If we act in the role of mentor, the role of "teacher" or "guide" as revealed in Homer's "Odyssey," we operate under a different set of beliefs. Our beliefs are most likely that the mentee wants us to give advice, that we have been down a similar path, and that our experiences translate to that of the mentee.

This gives us a feeling of value, worth, and wisdom. We take actions like talking more than listening, consulting, advising, and solving problems.

Again, not necessarily a negative. However, we will create a reality where we are the teacher, and the mentee is the student. They will most likely rely on us to have the answers.

A coach operates under an entirely different set of beliefs than a boss or a mentor. Like an Uber driver, when we act as a coach, we believe the coachee knows where he or she wants to go. I believe there are at least eight beliefs or assumptions a coach must operate under to experience the level of interaction we seek from coaching. These beliefs are aligned with widely accepted presuppositions discussed in the world of Neuro-Linguistic Programming (NLP).

When we hold to these beliefs, these presuppositions, we have a much easier time acting like a coach and seeing the incredible results of coaching and the Interaction principle.

Belief #1: Better solutions result when we come into a conversation in a state of not knowing.

Coaches simply stay curious; they do not enter a conversation with a predetermined solution but rather seek to learn more.

Belief #2: People respond to their view of reality, not to reality itself.

A coach meets someone where he or she is, without judgment, to see the world through the coachee's eyes. A coachee may believe that "everyone is out to get them." Though we may see the absurdity in the thought, we have to meet them there, judgement free, before we can help them move forward.

Belief #3: The more choices we have, the more control and ownership we feel.

People often come to a conversation to express problems. I have one friend who frequently calls me on her commute home, complaining about the traffic. I once gave her five wonderful solutions—leave earlier, leave later, take another route, work from home, or find another job— but she didn't want to hear any of those. A better approach would have been for her to determine her own, wonderful solutions and then pick the one that worked best. As I mentioned earlier, when we are doing all of the talking, the other person is not learning or changing. In fact, a good friend and mentor of mine uses the acronym WAIT (Why Am I Talking?) to help her remember to listen and ask rather than tell.

Belief #4: People are best motivated by a compelling vision.

Coaches put this principle to work by having the coachee articulate what they really want. Experts in marketing are experts at motivating people with a compelling vision. They help us see ourselves as taller, thinner, younger, smarter, sexier, etc. The result? We spend money!

Belief #5: People have the resources they need. This belief often stumps the leaders I work with. In their minds, the threat is that if people already have all the resources they need, then the leader isn't really needed. But what it really means is that the leader is one of those resources, but only one. Yes, leaders should be able to go on vacation without interruption, and the office continue to run. So, instead of rushing in to solve the problem or repair the situation, a leader who coaches holds back. They don't rush in to solve but rather help the coachee discover what resources are already available and how to best use them. And, what resources are missing and how to go find them.

Belief #6: The presenting problem is usually not the real problem.

When I was a director, one of my team members came into my office one day complaining about an email from one of her teammates. As I probed further, it was clear the email was only the presenting problem; the real problem was that she felt like the team did not value her opinion. A leader who coaches doesn't fall for the presenting problem. A coach stays curious, always digging deeper to find the real challenge.

Only by finding the real challenges can we help the coachee discover the best solutions.

Belief #7: There is a reward for all of our choices, actions, and behaviors.

All of these beliefs, or presuppositions, raise eyebrows, but this one trumps them all. I had a client just yesterday ask, "how could I possibly get a reward out of staying on this team?" The reality is we don't continue to do anything we don't receive some kind of reward or satisfaction from. This belief is not saying the reward is always a good reward. In the case of my client, perhaps her reward for staying was that she could continue to feel superior, complain and blame, play small, or avoid taking risks. The client has to discover what the reward is. The coach must simply remember there is a reward.

Belief #8: Tell them, they comply. Involve them, they commit.

When we can participate in creating something, we have a commitment to it. As an example, I think about two contrasting leaders. One was a boss in the purest sense of the word; it was "my way or the highway," and we all complied. The other leader was a mentor and coach who valued our experiences and opinions, and she involved us in all aspects of the team's activities. We were committed. In fact, we were so loyal to her that we willingly put in the extra hours necessary to see a project to its completion without pay.

When individuals in an organization, particularly leaders, operate off these eight beliefs, the culture becomes a culture of coaching. People stay curious, they listen and ask questions, they give courageous feedback and they seek to develop and improve performance both individually and collectively. When you consider your culture, what opportunities might open up if it operated as a coaching culture? What problems might disappear?

To truly integrate the Interaction principle, we must adopt the beliefs of a coach. But we must also actively develop the skills of coaching. To effectively coach, it is critical that we foster trust, develop a coaching presence, actively listen, and ask generative questions that illicit more information, insight, and discovery. To help us see what that looks like lived out, we can look to the International Coaching Federation (ICF), the premier accrediting body for certified professional coaches.

Foster trust

The Challenge chapter focused on building trust, and throughout this book, the impact of threat has been a common theme. If we want to promote a coaching culture and we want to experience the power of coaching, we must actively build trust. The ICF describes a healthy coaching relationship as one of mutual respect, safety, and support. Establishing trust, requires that the coach:

- shows genuine concern for the coachee's welfare and future;
- continuously demonstrates personal integrity, honesty, and sincerity;
- demonstrates respect for the coachee's perceptions, learning style, and personal being;
- provides ongoing support for and champions new behaviors and actions, including those involving risk-taking and fear of failure; and
- asks permission to coach in sensitive, new areas.

Coaching presence

This skill is defined by ICF as "the ability to be fully conscious and create spontaneous relationship with the client, employing a style that is open, flexible, and confident." Coaching presence can be difficult to achieve in today's world of overwhelming, continuous distractions. To effectively be present in all scenarios, a coach must:

- be present and flexible during the coaching process, an ability called "dancing in the moment;"
- access and trust one's own intuition, "go with the gut;"
- stay open to not knowing and taking risks;
- see many ways to work with the coachee and choose, in the moment, what is most effective;
- use humor effectively to create lightness and energy;
- confidently shift perspectives and experiment with new possibilities for one's own action; and
- demonstrate confidence in working with strong emotions and self-manage by not being overpowered or enmeshed with the coachee's emotions.

If we are to have this level of coaching presence, it is vital that the coach give the coachee his/her full, undivided attention, even if that means closing the laptop, turning off the phone, closing the door, or relocating the conversation.

Actively listen

In my experience, if we were to rate our level of listening on a scale of 1-10, most of us listen below a 5 (where we listen to respond, give an obligatory head nod, or offer encouraging affirmation). This is usually facade listening, the kind where the voices chattering in your head often have more to offer than the person talking to you. I've often heard this level of listening described as that of the foot tapper who really wants to respond, "Could you hurry up, so I can solve your problem and get on with my day?"

I encourage individuals who want the most out of coaching and the principle of Interaction to level-up their listening. When we are attending at higher levels on the continuum, we aren't listening to respond; rather, we are listening to truly understand. We aren't listening to solve a problem or give advice; we are waiting to ask the next great question. We aren't in "giving-and-telling" mode but rather in "discovering-and-learning" mode. If clients are struggling with this concept, I encourage them to block out 15 minutes every day to just practice level-up listening. The more they do it, the easier and more comfortable it becomes.

Level-up listening, also known as active listening, is very different from the way most of us typically attend to a conversation. Typical listening usually involves one of three responses.

How would you respond if a co-worker walked into your office, shut the door, and said she was so frustrated with someone who is a peer to both of you. What if she emphatically said, "I can't work with him anymore. He's driving me crazy!"

If you were at a typical listening level, you might fuel the fire by joining her complaint party with, "Girl, I know that's right! He's driving me crazy, too. I know just what you're talking about. I can't even believe he still has a job here."

Or, you might diminish her experience by playing the devil's advocate: "Well, he's been under a lot of stress lately. I don't think he meant to make you angry. He's a really nice guy." In that instance, you've taken a "power-over" rather than a "power-with" approach and forgotten to operate under the belief that people respond to their view of reality. You would have completely minimized her experience and made her feel that being frustrated was wrong.

A third typical listening level would lead you to solve her problem or give her advice. In that instance, which is a default response for most of us, you might say, "Well, you just need to tell him."

All these responses are typical, below-Level-5 listening. In contrast, level-up listening would require a coach to:

- attend to the coachee's agenda and not to the coach's agenda;
- hear the coachee's concerns, goals, values, and beliefs about what is and what is not possible;
- distinguish between the words, the tone of voice; and the body language;
- summarize, paraphrase, reiterate, and mirror what the coachee said to ensure clarity and understanding;

- encourage, accept, explore, and reinforce the coachee's expression of feelings, perceptions, concerns, beliefs, and suggestions;
- integrate and build on the coachee's ideas and suggestions;
- "bottom-line" or understand the essence of the coachee's communication and help him/her get there rather than engaging in long, descriptive stories; and
- allow the coachee to vent or "clear" the situation without judgment or attachment in order to move to next step(s).

Essentially, level-up listening is meeting people where they are without judgment or encouragement, staying curious and attentive, and not rushing ahead to a solution. So in our scenario, a level-up response may simply require rephrasing, such as, "So, John is frustrating you to the point that you don't think you can work with him anymore. Did I get that right?"

Generative questioning

Coaches must have the ability to ask questions that generate more information, insight, and discovery. This is a skill the ICF calls "powerful questioning," a competency they define as "the ability to ask questions that reveal the information needed for maximum benefit to the coaching relationship and to the coach." Like listening, asking generative or powerful questions doesn't always come naturally.

Most of us are accustomed to asking non-generative, or "typical," questions.

Let's contrast the two.

A <u>typical</u> question is closed-ended:
> *"You said you were frustrated?"*

A <u>generative</u> question is open-ended:
> *"I can sense your frustrated. Tell me more."*

A <u>typical</u> question looks backward:
> *"Tell me what happened?"*

A <u>generative</u> question looks forward:
> *"What is your ideal outcome?"*

A <u>typical</u> question seeks one solution:
> *"What are you going to do?"*

A <u>generative</u> question seeks many solutions:
> *"What are ways you could address the situation?"*

A <u>typical</u> question asks why:
> *"Why do you think he is doing that?"*

A <u>generative</u> question asks what or how:
> *"How is the frustration impacting the team?"*

A <u>typical</u> question includes nested advice:
> *"Have you thought about going to his supervisor?"*

A <u>generative</u> question encourages exploration:
> *"What is your go-forward plan?"*

A <u>typical</u> question places blame:
> *"Why is he being like that?"*

A <u>generative</u> question promotes accountability:
> *"How could you lessen your frustration?"*

Powerful questioning, as described by ICF involves:

- Asking questions that reflect active listening and an understanding of the coachee's perspective;

Interaction

- Asking questions that evoke discovery, insight, commitment or action (e.g., those that challenge the coachee's assumptions)
- Asking open-ended questions that create greater clarity, possibility or new learning
- Asking questions that move the coachee toward what they desire, not questions that ask the coachee to justify or look backward.

A coaching culture requires that all individuals, but particularly leaders, adopt the underlying beliefs about coaching as well as continuously seek to develop critical coaching skills. At a minimum, when we coach, we must be mindful of building a trust relationship, staying fully present, listening with intensity, and asking powerful, generative questions. By doing so, we can fully leverage the power of coaching and the power of the Interaction principle.

There are two specific situations in which using coaching to increase interaction, engagement, and ownership can give leaders a tremendous competitive advantage. One is in giving and receiving regular, ongoing feedback; coaching creates the perfect situation in which to have real-time, continuous conversations about wins, challenges, and performance. A second is when we need to have a direct, tough conversation with high courage and high consideration. A coaching approach to difficult conversations not only leads to better results but can also strengthen relationships.

Ongoing feedback

One of the biggest challenges leaders face is having continuous, ongoing conversations about the things that matter most. The days of having an "annual" review are over, especially with the Millennial Generation. As Gallup has discovered, Millennials have grown up with "right now" communication and feedback via the likes of Twitter, Instagram, and Snapchat, and they expect nothing less of their leadership. They aren't interested in receiving feedback once a year; they want to continuously interact and share their opinions and ideas.

Coaching is the perfect tool for providing that level of interaction.

Businessman and entrepreneur Quint Studer is well-known in the healthcare industry for promoting a leadership practice called "rounding." Inspired by the way physicians make rounds to check on patients, Studer recommended a similar approach for leaders to "round" with staff. This is a brilliant strategic practice that requires a very small time investment when compared with the big returns the leader gains in encouraging a true coaching culture.

Through meeting frequently with each individual and asking targeted questions, rounding can head problems off at the pass, provide people with the resources they need when they need them, recognize and appreciate team members, and gauge the "top-of-mind" concerns of the team.

A similar practice for encouraging interaction and feedback is one we teach called CHEC-ins, based on an acronym for connect, help, empower, and commit. CHEC-ins are:

- regular, intentional, yet casual and non-threatening conversations;
- conducted one-on-one with each team member to increase feedback, ownership, and accountability;
- positive and forward-focused conversations to improve individual and collective work performance;
- centered around the team members' ideas, needs, and concerns; and
- a safe place to encourage interaction and two-way communication.

CHEC-ins should occur as frequently as necessary, depending on the needs of the team. Some leaders conduct them daily, some weekly, and others monthly. To effectively facilitate a CHEC-in, the leader utilizes the critical coaching skills of building trust, staying present, listening with intensity, and asking generative questions.

Connect

The idea behind this initial step is to lower threat and increase trust by making a comfortable, personal connection.

Example:

> *"Hi Jill. How did your daughter's soccer game go last weekend?"*

203

Help

Now is the optimal time to focus on level-up listening and asking generative questions to identify what challenges are present and how you can help.

Examples:

> *"What challenges are showing up?"*
>
> *"Out of the demands right now, which are most disruptive?"*
>
> *"When you think of your projects, where are you encountering obstacles?"*
>
> *"How can I best support you?"*
>
> *"Of the people you have interacted with, who has been particularly helpful?"*
>
> *"What can I do today (this week) to help you move forward?"*

Empower

Once you are clear on the concerns, use powerful, generative questions to engage the team member in identifying solutions.

Examples:

> *"You mentioned tight deadlines as being a challenge. What recommendations do you have?"*
>
> *"What have you seen work previously?"*
>
> *"How do you suggest we communicate these suggestions to the team?"*

Commit

The fourth step is to recap the situation and look at next steps to ensure everyone is clear and on target to follow through. This is also the perfect time to set up the next CHEC-in.

Example:

> *"So, just to be clear, I'm going to talk with IT about login requirements, and you will bring up the security alert at our team meeting this afternoon. Did I get that right? Great. Let's follow-up next Monday to discuss if we have seen improvement."*

Another common situation where coaching and engaging the principle of Interaction is particularly useful is when we need to have tough conversations. After all, if we truly want coaching cultures where all members are invited to participate in coaching, then everyone involved needs to have an approach for addressing the tough talks with high courage, and high consideration. When people utilize the four critical coaching skills and have a framework for the conversation, they are much more willing to have it in the first place because it reduces threat and anxiety. In addition, they are much more likely to get positive results because all parties approach the conversation with a mindset of collaboration rather than one of competition.

The GROW model, a platform for having productive talks, is perfect for blending coaching skills, using a template, and encouraging interaction. GROW—which stands for goal, reality, options, and what's next—is an excellent template for lowering resistance for tough talks but can also be used for multiple purposes including strategic planning. As the name indicates, the idea is to grow and move forward as you focus on the goal, take an honest look at reality, collaboratively explore solutions, and collectively agree on the best next steps.

Let's look at how your frustrated co-worker from the scenario discussed earlier could use GROW, along with coaching skills, to talk with John about what she is experiencing.

Goal

The first step is to clearly identify the goal, or desired outcome, of the conversation. What is the ultimate goal? What is the ideal outcome? What is a vision that is compelling to everyone involved?

Example:

> *"John, do you have a few minutes? I wanted to talk about how you and I can best support each other in hitting our sales targets."*

Reality

Next, you must objectively share your perception of reality. What is the current situation? What are a couple of specific things that are happening? What are you seeing? And what is the other person seeing?

Examples:

> *"Well, I'd like to share a couple of frustrations, and I want to hear what you are experiencing. Is that okay?"*
>
> *"Last week, I felt like you cut me off at our team meeting when I was sharing an idea. And today, I received an email from you with red, bold letters that made me think you were yelling at me. I don't want to jump to conclusions. Can you help me understand?"*

Options

Now it's time to explore ideas collaboratively. What are some ways to improve? What has worked in the past? What has never been tried?

Example:

> *"Let's brainstorm how can we move forward more productively? I have a few ideas, and I also want to hear your ideas."*

What's next?

Finally, restate next steps and be sure everyone involved is clear on what each is responsible for. This is also the best time to set the follow-up meeting.

Rule of thumb: never end a GROW conversation without a scheduling a follow-up GROW conversation on the calendar.

Example:

> *"Let's recap our next steps. I'm going to let you know immediately if I feel like you aren't listening. Your turn... Great! Let's follow up on Friday to see if we are seeing improvement or if we need to brainstorm some more options."*

Disclaimer: GROW is not a magic bullet. There have been times when I've coached leaders who led a textbook GROW conversation with a team member, brilliantly executed the critical coaching skills, and still had the employee leave. But, the win is that the leader modeled "power with," demonstrated a genuine interest in what the employee had to offer and provided a powerful example to that team member of what it looks like to value another human being's insight, ideas, and opinions.

In summary, the principle of Interaction is about staying curious, avoiding judgment, and believing that possibilities are endless and that outcomes can exceed our expectations when we can co-create the solution. Interaction is about honoring people and empowering them to have both a choice and a voice. By involving rather than telling, and by discovering rather than solving, we grow ourselves, we grow our teams, and we move people from compliance to commitment.

Using Emotions

| leveraging the power of the emotional brain

Regardless of the industry, the profession, or the title, we are all in the relationship business.

It's the middle of the week at an online service company known for its focus on innovation and exemplary customer service.

On the first floor, in the training center, Trainer Mark is kicking off a leadership program for "high potentials." The first workshop for these emerging leaders begins today, and the focus is on leading with vision and values. Mark opens the class by having participants think about a leader they have had the privilege of knowing personally. Small groups discuss leaders who come to mind and a few reasons why, while someone from each table notes the characteristics that made these leaders great on a flipchart.

Unforgettable Leadership

Cathy's office is just down the hall. As VP of sales for almost 10 years, she has built a solid, high-performing team. They are frequently visible in the community, going to baseball games, bowling, or volunteering in a local homeless shelter. One of Cathy's managers has recently returned from maternity leave, and Cathy has noticed how tired she looks and the angst on her face after she leaves her newborn at day care. Cathy calls the manager into her office. The woman hesitantly walks in and sits in front of her boss' desk. Cathy says, "You know, Susan, I've been thinking. We can craft a flexible work schedule for a while, if that's something you would be interested in." Susan smiles with tears in her eyes.

Raul works on the second floor, the newest member of the call center. He receives a call from one of the guys out in the field who is having difficulty logging into his account. Raul immediately gives the technician the code he needs, and while waiting for the system to connect, they spend a few minutes reliving the last 60 seconds of their local basketball team's championship game. Raul's supervisor walks by as Raul is ending the call, gives him a high five, and says, "Great job on that call. We're glad you're on the team."

Sandra is backing up her delivery truck at the service entrance to the company's cafeteria. She worked on a manufacturing line for nearly 20 years but always wanted to run her own business; Sandra came from a long line of entrepreneurs and always had a hunch she had inherited that entrepreneurial spirit. She loved to bake; even as a little girl, she would make cupcakes and muffins for her classmates.

About five years ago, Sandra took a tremendous risk and put her life's savings on the line to begin her bakery. Business was slow but steady at first, then she landed her first big corporate contract with the online service company just down the road from her small shop. Sandra was thrilled when she was awarded the contract to provide fresh-baked goods to this organization. She remembers it like yesterday, jumping up and down in celebration with her one part-time employee. Nothing gives her more joy than to do what she loves and to use her gift to help others have a better day.

Around the corner from the cafeteria is the founder's office. Peter is a legend in the community who attended a prestigious military academy and went on to build countless successful businesses. A true philanthropist, he financially supports multiple community initiatives including the symphony hall, a museum, and a center for excellence in research. Though Peter is not involved in the day-to-day business of the company, he still maintains office hours, welcomes all new hires, and holds frequent conversations with employees. Today, he is hosting a young high school student who aspires to attend the military academy Peter attended. He welcomes the young man to his office and closes the door, and they begin to discuss steps the young man needs to take in order to fulfill his dream.

Bob walks by Peter's door just as it is closing and chuckles. He passes Andrew, who asks him, "Hey Bob, would you be able to help me with a new product design?" Bob says, "Absolutely. Any time on Friday works for me." As Andrew is walking away, Bob says, "Hey, wait just a second. I'm going to send you a couple of links to sites I think may be helpful. Take a look at them when you can. Also, Sonia just started with us a couple of weeks ago, and her work is brilliant. How about we get her in on this project as well?" Andrew says, "Sounds great. Look for the invite, and I'll see you on Friday."

On the third floor, Lisa welcomes her team as they arrive for their weekly meeting. Before she begins with the agenda, she expresses her sincere appreciation for all of the hard work the entire team put in to meet an important deadline, specifically recognizing two people who came in over the weekend to make sure all of the final materials were ready to ship. The team cheers, claps, and whistles. Linda tells them how honored she is to lead such a high-performing team then gives the floor over to Carlos to discuss the first agenda item.

Overview

The principle of this chapter, Using Emotion, acknowledges that emotions, rather than logic, run the show. Or, as other brain-based learning experts have expressed, emotions "seal the deal." If we want to work with rather than against how the brain works best, we must recognize the powerful role emotions play in our own lives and in the lives of those we seek to lead and influence.

It is true that we aren't thinking individuals who happen to feel. We simply aren't driven and motivated by facts and figures, at least not in the long-term. The truth is quite the opposite: emotion is what drives people to move from the possible to the impossible, from where they are to where they want to be.

We are emotional individuals who happen to think.

This human element cannot be ignored. But it can make things messy and complex. There's a common saying among leaders, "Business is easy until people get involved." If we could remove the human element, most of the problems we encounter would not exist.

We've all been there. The strategy that sounded flawless in theory and looked perfectly simple on paper but fell into chaos during implementation. It reminds me of a scene in the film, *Miracle on the Hudson,* in which US Airways pilot Chesley "Sully" Sullenberger saves 155 lives by landing a plane on the Hudson River after a flock of Canadian geese strikes both engines. Despite his heroic deed, the National Transportation Safety Board questioned Sully's decision, proposing he had time to safely land the plane at nearby LaGuardia airport. To test their hypothesis, they used a flight simulator.

As the birds simulate hitting the engines, the simulator pilots calmly acknowledge the birds and turn left. In that simulation, the plane could have made it to the airport, but what the simulator doesn't account for is the human element. In real life, the brain must process a complicated wave of emotions along with the facts: What the heck just happened? What options do we have? We are responsible for 155 lives, or we may die.

Unlike in the simulator, making an immediate decision under duress requires time, logic, and emotion—the greatest, most unpredictable variable of all.

Great leaders and organizations do not resist emotions that drive the human element; they embrace them. They don't work against emotion but rather work with emotion. They fully agree with Dan and Chip Heath's conclusion in their book, *Switch: How to Change Things When Change is Hard.* If we want to people to change, grow, be motivated, and learn, then we simply must put feeling first.

Cultures that fail to put feeling first:

- are toxic and dysfunctional;
- have leaders and teams who are unwilling to be vulnerable;
- tolerate and even reward leaders who are self-centered and ego-driven;
- foster an environment of learned helplessness;
- have a higher rate of sickness and depression;
- suffer from employees who hoard information for fear that if they share, they lose their worth and their job;
- do not act in alignment with their vision and values;

- are typically high-threat rather than high-trust;
- create teams that operate as a group of individuals rather than as a united front;
- often cover up mistakes rather than take responsibility for them;
- maintain the status quo;
- act conventionally;
- fill positions with little thought for passion or strengths;
- have a low tolerance for innovation or risk-taking;
- coach for punitive reasons only;
- do not foster a community of loyalty and commitment;
- are quick to blame and criticize, and are slow to hold themselves and others accountable; and
- tolerate unacceptable, unprofessional behavior.

These cultures suffer unnecessary costs. Their emphasis is not on building highly functioning and committed relationships. They do not honor the human element. Therefore, they create excessive people problems. Cultures that recognize the power of emotion and use this principle have a very different look and feel.

Cultures in which feeling comes first:

- are healthy and provide an environment where people can grow and develop;
- have leaders and teams who are willing to be vulnerable without fear of retribution;

Unforgettable Leadership

- reward leaders who invest in themselves and their teams;
- foster an environment of accountability and ownership;
- have higher levels of employee satisfaction and retention;
- freely share information and promote collaboration;
- give credit where credit is due;
- are characterized by high-trust relationships with teammates and customers;
- own up to mistakes and stay curious on ways to prevent them in the future;
- see development and feedback as a gift;
- challenge the status quo;
- put the right people in the right jobs;
- consider unconventional ways of meeting challenges;
- have a high tolerance for innovation and risk-taking;
- coach for development and have meaningful conversations about goals and performance throughout the year;
- enjoy the benefits of loyalty and commitment;
- are slow to blame and criticize, and are quick to hold themselves and others accountable; and
- have clearly communicated expectations and zero tolerance for unacceptable, unprofessional behavior.

Cultures where emotions and relationships are embraced reap the benefits because of their awareness. They are the organizations that survive financial crises, attract the top talent, and lead in their industry. They honor the human element and realize that individuals are driven by passion, emotion, and feeling. They intentionally build on strengths and are as concerned with healthy people as they are a healthy bottom line. They have significantly fewer people problems.

Reflection

- If a personal acquaintance described your strengths as a leader, what might he/she say?
- If someone who has worked closely with you described your strengths as a team member, what might he/she say?
- Describe a situation in which you were successful in managing yourself.
- Describe a situation in which you were not successful in managing yourself.
- When was the last time you were effective in influencing others?
- What is the most memorable classroom learning experience you've ever had? What are some things that make that memory stand out?

Using the charts below, rate how frequently you exhibit the following behaviors, then rate how you believe others would rate you on a scale of one to four.

You

	1	2	3	4
I know when I'm becoming defensive.				
I welcome constructive criticism.				
I give credit where credit is due.				
I cope with stress in a healthy, effective way.				
I willingly admit my mistakes.				
I immediately look for the good in changes.				
I remain calm in a crisis.				
I am part of the solution and not part of the problem.				
I do all that is expected of me without being told.				
I create opportunities.				
I proactively stop ineffective behaviors.				
I act in alignment with my values.				
I put my whole heart into everything I do.				
I respect the decisions of my authorities.				
I confront situations that need to be confronted.				

Using Emotions

Others

	1	2	3	4
I listen to understand and do not respond.				
I do not judge others.				
I detect others' unspoken needs.				
People see me as trustworthy.				
I encourage others.				
I challenge conventional ways of thinking.				
I seek out people whose perspectives are different from my own.				
I see the potential in people.				
I seek feedback from people around me.				
I model the behavior I want to see in others.				
I avoid mind reading and making assumptions.				
I hold others accountable.				
I protect and promote my team's reputation.				
I promote a collaborative and friendly environment.				
I go above and beyond without needing praise or recognition.				

Neurology & Science

The principle of Using Emotion increases returns, loyalty, and profits while decreasing problems and costs. It follows with how the brain works best. To paraphrase the great philosophical band Van Halen, we are simply humans being. And in our being human, emotions are the accelerating ingredient. As Shawn Achor says, we enjoy a competitive advantage, a happiness advantage, when our brain is on positive and we engage positive emotions.

Emotions

Ever had a "no-matter-what" moment? Those are the defining, often life-changing instances when, "no matter what," you were going to accomplishing something. Perhaps it was about making a change. Several years ago, I went through a devastating personal crisis and vowed that "no matter what," I was going to get out of debt and stay there. And I did. Maybe your moment focused on achieving a goal? I remember I was fiercely determined to finish my doctorate coursework, even though it landed me in the hospital with severe headaches and fatigue. But I did it. Or was your moment directed at making a major life move? I remember the day almost 18 years ago, I decided, while driving in rush-hour traffic, to leave the company I worked for and start my own business.

No. Matter. What.

I have found in my coaching that everyone has a "no-matter-what" story, like running a marathon, or beating cancer, or going vegan, or getting a promotion. We all have that "thing" inside us that motivates and fuels us to accomplish the goal that, at first, may have seemed impossible.

What is that "thing?" It's passion, it's desire, it's... emotion. Let's return to the Big Deals discussed earlier and reinforced throughout this book:

Big Deal #1: your prefrontal cortex is priceless; it is the seat of thought, analysis, good decision-making, speech, willpower, and self-control.

Big Deal #2: threat to the brain is threat to the brain. Nothing can shut down the PFC like threat. And your brain decides what it perceives is threat. So, whether it's a poisonous snake or a poisonous comment hurled at you, your brain will respond in a very similar way (if it perceives the snake and the comment as threat).

Now, here's Big Deal #3: emotions run the show. Emotions are very much like an accelerating ingredient that can fuel the PFC and allow us to accomplish those "no-matter-what" moments and function at our very best. Or, emotions can fuel threat and allow us to have what I call "freak-show" moments, where we function at our very worst.

Let's say two leaders are leading change initiatives involving merging two companies, one with a strong revenue stream and healthy culture, the other with a weak revenue stream and toxic culture. One year into the merger, the economy dives. Profits fall, and shareholders panic. Talent leaves in droves. Internal complaints and lawsuits build. One leader is filled with fear and paralyzed with threat; she looks for the nearest exit and takes the first job offer that comes her way. The other leader, however, sees the situation as a challenge. He makes deep cuts, creates a guiding team, lays out a strategic plan for recovery, rebuilds the organization, and sets the company on a course for unprecedented success. For the first leader, threat was accelerated by emotion. For the other, challenge was accelerated by emotion.

The same happens early in life. Imagine two 10-year-old baseball players playing for two different teams on two different fields. Both teams are down by one point, and the bases are loaded, with a runner on third and two outs. Both boys are up at bat on their respective fields, keenly aware that the win or loss rests on their shoulders. One player stands at the plate and freezes, striking out. The other player digs in and dominates, hitting a grand slam. What is threat to one brain may be challenge to another. Emotion fuels both.

Emotion is also an accelerating ingredient in learning and behavior change. If there is no emotion involved in learning, there is no learning. If we want a learning experience of any kind—a class, webinar, presentation, or meeting—to be transformational and impact performance, we must engage emotion. We simply cannot stand and tell facts and figures. We must engage people on an emotional level.

Using Emotions

While we still have a great deal to discover about the brain, we know the emotional brain was ignored for a long time in brain research. In fact, many once believed that information entered through the "thinking" part of the brain and, like so many corporations, the information was disseminated throughout the organization accordingly. So many of our educational models and leadership models and cultural beliefs are based on that way of thinking. That we are fact-driven creatures.

Still today, teachers, professors, trainers, and team leaders often stand in front of a group, spewing facts, figures, rules, and processes, and wonder why no one remembers anything they say, let alone make a change because of it. Company presidents stand before teams enduring hardships in times of change and, in a darkened room, talk to slides with charts. Parents lecture children at the dinner table about the dangers of smoking, drinking, and drugs, then tell them not to do it. In each case, the speakers wonder why people aren't motivated to learn and marvel that they continue to resist change. All that communication is a waste of time and energy if we fail to trigger emotion. For, we are feeling-driven creatures.

Scientists such as Joseph LeDoux have helped us shift our thinking in a way as dramatic as the Copernican Revolution (the paradigm shift that said no, the earth isn't stationary in space with the sun revolving around us; the earth revolves around the sun). Thanks to brain research, we now know that humans are emotional individuals who happen to think. Information is largely processed in the emotional center of the brain involving a complex area called the limbic system. To put it simply, emotions can "wake up" the prefrontal cortex and propel us to achieve greatness, or they can "shut down" the PFC and "fire up" threat and prevent us from achieving greatness.

There are steps we can take to minimize the latter impact, such as being mindful of how threat impacts our brains and what triggers seem to activate it. We call these triggers the "yellow lights." The analogy is powerful: if you are approaching an intersection and the light is yellow, it's in your best interest to slow down and pay close attention to traffic around you; yes, you may be able to speed up and blow through the intersection without consequence, but there is also a good chance that if you ignore the yellow light, your vehicle could be T-boned. Gaining self-awareness, then, requires us to identify and become extremely present to our own "yellow lights."

For years, recovery groups created ways to help people tune into their "yellow lights" or triggers, using memorable acronyms like the popular HALT. For example, many of us are particularly vulnerable to emotional hijackings when we find ourselves Hungry, Angry, Lonely, and/or Tired. And who is most likely to deal with us when we are hungry, angry, lonely, and tired? Ironically, the most important people in our lives: our friends and families.

It's important that we learn strategies for recognizing and "turning down the dial" on threat. Obviously, it's harmful to our brains and impacts our lives. Cognitive researcher Sian Beilock writes brilliantly about the science behind why some brains may "choke" under high pressure or in high threat situations while others do not. But as we are learning to "turn down the dial" on threat, we also need to be mindful of how to "turn up the dial" on emotion, especially positive emotion, which gives the brain a competitive edge.

Positive emotion

Positive psychology, most often attributed to the work of Martin Seligman, is one of the most exciting fields of studies when it comes to the power of emotion. Rather than deficits, positive psychology looks at strengths. Rather than focusing on what is broken, positive psychology sees what is working well. And rather than approach mental health from a disease model, positive psychology approaches it from a wellness model.

Negative emotions can be crippling, and we are hardwired to notice and remember the negative. Negative emotions elevate cortisol for an extended period of time. Positive emotions, on the other hand, have a short life as the release of dopamine only lasts briefly, sometimes milliseconds. We tend to hang on to bad experiences too long and not hang on to good experiences long enough. Accessing positive emotion and using it as a competitive advantage is an intentional shift we must monitor and practice. However, the results are worth the effort.

Positive psychology tells us our brains work more effectively when they are set to positive than when they are set to negative. 30-35% more effectively. It's sort of like playing a mental game of I Spy. If someone says I spy something blue, we automatically look for blue. When we mentally think I spy negative, we automatically scan the world for the negative.

We know that while focusing on threat and negativity may help our survival at times, it also limits our ability to think creatively and see all options to solving problems. Negative thinking actually narrows our visual field. We simply don't "see" as much—literally and figuratively. Optimism, on the other hand, elevates all the good chemicals such as dopamine, serotonin, and norepinephrine. These are critical chemicals we need to focus, have higher levels of creativity and energy, and stay flexible and open to new ideas and learning. Additionally, optimism activates the brain's reward system. When we mentally think I spy positive, we automatically scan the world for the positive.

Unfortunately, scanning for the positive does not come naturally for brains that have operated for thousands of years on negative hardwiring, looking for what could go wrong or what could kill us. And we know willpower, powered in the prefrontal cortex, is a limited resource. Therefore, we need to adopt strategies beyond trying harder and having more discipline.

Shawn Achor in his book, The Happiness Advantage, offers specific suggestions for having more happiness, gratitude, and optimism. He encourages meditation, which activates the left prefrontal cortex, a part of the brain that ignites when we feel happy. He suggests finding something to look forward to; our brains actually get a bigger charge from the reward system as they anticipate the reward rather than when they receive it. Sometimes I enjoy thinking about my upcoming vacation as much, or perhaps more, than actually experiencing the trip. And, we've all known or heard of people who achieve a long-held dream, only to fall into a deep depression once it is accomplished. High performers always have the next something to look forward to in queue.

Achor suggests people serve others by intentionally committing what he calls conscious or random acts of kindness. We've all heard that it's better to give than to receive. In fact, a Chinese proverb states, "If you want happiness for a lifetime, help someone else." There is great value to the brain when we give to others. When we serve and volunteer, we activate the pleasure centers in our brain, the same areas that are activated by sex or food. According to Cleveland Clinic, this "helper's high" carries a number of health benefits. People who serve were more likely to have:

- lower blood pressure;
- increased self-esteem;
- less depression;
- lower stress levels;
- longer life;
- and, of course, greater happiness!

Achor also reinforces the importance of exercise for the brain. Activity increases the positive because it elevates blood flow to the brain, boosts good chemicals in the brain, and improves self-esteem and self-image. Like others, including Gallup, Achor emphasizes the importance of leveraging strengths. As discussed in the Relevance chapter, when we build on strengths, we activate the prefrontal cortex and accelerate positive emotions. The VIA Institute on Character offers a free strengths assessment that allows identification of our "Signature Strengths."

The more we use our inherent strengths, the happier we will be.

Finally, Achor encourages those seeking the happiness advantage to create a positive physical space. Jenny Quillien, author of "Clever Digs: How Workspaces Can Enable Thought," offers insightful information on how to design physical spaces that promote connectivity. Equally important is how we denote our positive energy space; the less negativity we are exposed to through social media, TV, and toxic people, the happier we will be.

And emotions really are contagious; work in the area of mirror neurons, though somewhat controversial, has allowed us to better understand why we can observe an action or sense a feeling in someone else and experience it ourselves. This is all the more reason why creating a healthy, positive culture not only benefits ourselves but also those we seek to influence.

Application

Perhaps, the principle of Using Emotion has its greatest application in the work of Emotional Intelligence. Early in my graduate studies, I was introduced to Harvard researcher Howard Gardner's work, called the "Multiple Intelligences" theory. It was the first time I had ever considered the idea that an IQ test only captured a close-up snapshot of someone's intelligence. Gardner's theory opened up a new world for me. He allowed me to understand the brain houses multiple intelligences, far beyond the traditional mathematical and linguistic intelligences captured on standardized tests. His approach meant I had a shot at being intelligent.

Gardner shifts the intelligence question. Rather than asking how smart is someone, Gardner challenges us to ask how each person is smart. That shift in questioning changed everything for me. What if we really approached development with this perspective? We would stop looking for the negatives and the deficits, and start searching for the strengths and the positives.

I quickly learned that Gardner's theory proposes intelligence can come in many forms—musical, spatial, naturalist, and bodily-kinesthetic—and all are as valuable as mathematical-logical intelligence and linguistic intelligence. In fact, Gardner redefined intelligence as the ability to create products or solve problems that are important and valuable to the culture.

So, once I realized intelligence is defined by needs of the culture, I began asking questions, such as, What if the culture is leadership? What intelligence counts the most when we are tasked to lead others? Creating resonance with teams? Managing relationships? According to work in Multiple Intelligence Theory, the two most valuable intelligences are those that aren't tested on a standardized test. They are called intrapersonal intelligence, the ability to know and manage self, and interpersonal intelligence, the ability to interact, connect, and influence others. These are the perfect foundation for emotional intelligence.

Utilizing the principle of emotion isn't touchy-feely or happy-clappy as some people I've worked with through the years initially believed. I recall a supervisor in one of my classes who declared that he always told his men to "leave their personal problems at home." Those antiquated ways of thinking are long gone. We now know that emotional intelligence is an essential competency for leaders. Daniel Goleman defines the abilities of emotional intelligence as the abilities to:

- Stay self-motivated;
- Persist during frustrating times;
- Control one's impulsivity;
- Delay immediate gratification;
- Manage one's moods;
- Demonstrate compassion;
- Maintain optimism;
- Express empathy and hope.

We live in a world where we see few examples of these abilities. Developing personal emotional intelligence is essential in a world full of violence, unpredictability, rapid change, uncertainties, and complexities.

I realize multiple, comprehensive books have been written on emotional intelligence theory from every angle. A variety of powerful assessments on the topic are available, and I highly recommend using an assessment for your own development, as well as that of your team. In fact, a quick Google search of "emotional intelligence theory" elicited more than 2.5 million results. My goal is not to explain emotional intelligence, but to use its behaviors to give a description of what the principle of Using Emotion looks like, lived out.

Emotional intelligence breaks down into two major categories of behaviors: those we see when someone is successfully managing himself/herself, and those we see when someone is effectively interacting with and influencing others. The order is important, for we cannot begin to positively impact and influence others if we are not first and foremost willing to do the hardest work of all: learn to recognize and manage emotions in ourselves.

Managing self

As you read the following descriptions, rate how frequently you and your team members exhibit these nine behaviors (1=Never, 2= Rarely, 3=Most of the time, 4= Always):

231

- **Self-awareness**: Leaders and teams who are self-aware are fully present and mindful, able to identify the triggers or "yellow-lights" before they have power over their behavior. They know when they become defensive and territorial, know how their behavior impacts others, and keep situations and events in perspective without overreacting.

Self rating: ___

Team rating: ___

- **Self-management**: Leaders and teams who are self-managing see the giving and receiving of feedback as valuable gifts. They continuously assess their weaknesses and strengths both individually and collectively. They capitalize on situations where they can use their strengths. They are not shy about asking for help.

Self rating: ___

Team rating: ___

- **Self-confidence**: Leaders and teams who are self-confident are vulnerable with each other. They are as confident in discussing their weaknesses as they are their strengths. They hold themselves accountable and responsible, and they avoid passing the blame. When mistakes are made, they actively learn from them and quickly move forward. They give credit where credit is due.

Self rating: ___

Team rating: ___

- **Self-control**: Leaders and teams who have self-control know the point of no return. They know how far they can push themselves and others. They know their triggers, manage their negative emotions appropriately, and have strategies for dealing with stress and pressure. They are mindful and intentional, and they think before they act.

Self rating: ___

Team rating: ___

● **Transparency**: Leaders and teams who are transparent are known for their reliability and consistency. They follow through on promises and communicate quickly when they are unable to deliver. They are willing to openly admit mistakes and faults. They are willing to stay the course despite opposition when they believe the right decision has been made.

Self rating: ___

Team rating: ___

Adaptability: Leaders and teams who are adaptable realize that people don't resist change, they resist confusion. Therefore, they seek answers and solutions in times of change rather than become rattled or upset. They respect the decisions of the authorities who lead them, even if they do not agree. They search for the good in changes.

Self rating: ___

Team rating: ___

Achievement: Leaders and teams who are achievers not only set goals, they set the right goals. They remain calm, strategic, and focused when obstacles surface. They are not discouraged by the words or actions of others, and they are willing to have the tough conversations with high courage and high consideration.

Self rating: ___

Team rating: ___

Initiative: Leaders and teams who take initiative see themselves as owners. They have an entrepreneurial spirit and mindset. They work in their business, and they work on their business. They are quick to address and stop ineffective behaviors and hold themselves and others accountable. They create opportunities rather than waiting for them. They offer solutions when there are problems. They meet expectations without being told or reminded to do so.

Self rating: ___

Team rating: ___

Optimism: Leaders and teams who are optimistic leverage the power of positivity. When setbacks or disappointments happen, they deal with them constructively while maintaining a positive outlook. They create a positive environment for those around them. They see purpose in their calling.

Self rating: ___

Team rating: ___

Influencing others

Clearly, the behaviors necessary for effectively influencing others rely on the behaviors of managing self. Intrapersonal and interpersonal intelligence go hand-in-hand. Indeed, if we are not wholeheartedly committed to growing and developing ourselves, we have no capacity and actually no right to influence others.

As you read the following descriptions, how frequently would you rate how you and your team exhibit these nine behaviors (1=Never, 2= Rarely, 3=Most of the time, 4= Always):

● <u>Empathy</u>: Leaders and teams who embrace empathy are highly self-managing. Therefore, they have the awareness and the resources available when others need help. They genuinely care about others as human beings and are committed to listening to better understand rather than rush in and offer solutions. They truly consider others' perspectives, seek to avoid judgment, and hold unconditional positive regard for others.

Self rating: ___

Team rating: ___

● <u>Service</u>: Leaders and teams who demonstrate service go the extra mile. They are willing to put others ahead of themselves if necessary and consider the opportunity to support and serve a privilege. They evaluate the impact of their decisions and commitments on those who depend on them. They not only meet the spoken need but detect the underlying, unspoken needs of others as well. No task is too menial.

Self rating: ___

Team rating: ___

- **Inspiration**: Leaders and teams who inspire give life. They are encouragers and energizers. They realize emotions are contagious, and they seek to spread enthusiasm and passion. They continuously see the potential in people, in new opportunities, and in times of change. They are frequently sought out by others because of their contagious spirit.

  Self rating: ___

  Team rating: ___

- **Change catalyst**: Leaders and teams who are change catalysts not only are adaptable when change comes, they lead the change initiative. They seek opportunities for change and are always challenging the status quo and conventional methods. They are not content with the way things have always been if there is a possibility for improvement. They remain optimistic, visionary, and open to different perspectives and insights in times of change.

  Self rating: ___

  Team rating: ___

- **Developing others**: Leaders and teams who develop others do so not for selfish gain but because they truly want to be a part of someone else's growth and journey. They see untapped potential in others and are willing to give of their time, share their experiences and knowledge, and invest in others without expecting anything in return. They freely share information if it can benefit someone else.

  Self rating: ___

  Team rating: ___

- <u>Situational awareness</u>: Leaders and teams who have situational awareness are mindful of the politics and agendas at work in any organization. They keep their ears and eyes open to the culture as well as to changes outside of their organization and industry. They stay curious, listen to understand, and ask questions to generate discovery and insight. They adapt easily to social networks and changing dynamics.

Self rating: ___

Team rating: ___

- **Influence**: Leaders and teams who seek to influence model the behavior they want to see from others. They are fully aware that influence and influenza come from the same root word. They communicate directly, giving a realistic, straightforward view of reality and do not inflate the truth to make it more attractive. They are committed to helping others move in a positive direction and are persuasive because of their commitment to their integrity.

Self rating: ___

Team rating: ___

- **Conflict management**: Leaders and teams who effectively manage conflict confront situations that need to be addressed in a timely manner. They can handle difficult situations, conversations, and people with diplomacy and tact. They focus on the goal and the real issue, not on personalities and opinions. They listen fully and ask questions to better see the situation from others' perspectives. They avoid mind-reading, making assumptions, and jumping to conclusions. They work to keep the solution closest to the problem and do not involve others unnecessarily.

Self rating: ___

Team rating: ___

● **Teamwork**: Leaders and teams who work together realize the sophisticated skills required to be a good team member and the importance of maintaining unity. They are loyal to each other and to their word. They honor the absent, and do not speak negatively of someone if he/she is not present to offer a defense. They actively seek ways to demonstrate appreciation for each other, and they reward and recognize achievements. They hold each other accountable for living out the team's vision and values. They promote a welcoming, friendly, and cooperative environment. They protect and promote the team's reputation with outsiders.

Self rating: ___

Team rating: ___

The stories shared at the beginning of this chapter are actual experiences I observed during my years consulting. The organization described successfully assembled a team of emotionally intelligent individuals, which resulted in emotionally intelligent leaders, teams, and culture. Their healthy profit and growth are a direct reflection of their healthy culture.

What they are experiencing is similar to what Goleman, McKee, and Boyatzis talk about in their book, *Primal*

Leadership. Not surprisingly, these authors discovered that those organizations with healthy, emotionally intelligent cultures enjoyed better business results. Then they asked an important question: if culture drives business results, what drives culture? Overwhelmingly, they found the number one influence on culture was the actions of one person: the leader.

Leaders who drive healthy cultures recognize the power of Using Emotion for themselves first and foremost, and then for those they seek to influence. They embrace the human element. They are forever mindful that we are individuals who have emotion and happen to think. They realize that they are in the relationship business.

Multiple Intelligences

| Embracing differences and sameness

Stop asking, "how smart are you?"
Start asking, "how are you smart?"

R uth sat in deep reflection at her first executive team meeting, one month after her hiring. When she initially walked in, there wasn't a chair for her at the table--literally. Though everyone was friendly and introduced themselves as the team gathered, she noticed one seat was missing: hers. So, she rolled over a chair from the room next door. The CEO gave her a warm introduction as the hospital system's Chief Diversity Officer, a newly appointed position. But when he asked if anyone had questions about Ruth or her role, the team was silent. Thirty minutes into the meeting, she realized it was dominated by three members. Each had a business background from the same university, had a long tenure with the company, and approached every situation from similar perspectives. Ruth noticed that a couple of team members had attempted to challenge their recommended solution but were quickly shot down. When a vote was taken to move to the next agenda item, the room was silent.

Ruth knew why this group needed a Chief Diversity Officer, but she was questioning whether they were truly committed to the changes that were necessary. As the meeting progressed, she began to reflect on her first 30 days since taking the position.

She was drawn to the hospital system because it served a diverse community. It provided health services in several neighborhoods with extreme economic differences; the population served ranged from young families to those in assisted living. Several large, global companies had recently relocated their headquarters to this city, bringing employees and their cultures from all over the world.

At her interview, Ruth received a tour of one of the group's busiest hospitals. She immediately took notice of the diversity of ages, economic backgrounds, and nationalities sitting in the waiting room. And yet, the staff diversity was not reflective of the people they served.

That day, Ruth saw a Spanish-speaking mother with a sick child who asked a staff member for directions to the lab. The employee did not speak Spanish, nor did he offer to find a translator. She also observed an Indian family grieving in a nearby room. Meanwhile, just outside the hospital, an older woman, looking very confused, was pushing her husband in a wheelchair.

Ruth sat in on a physicians' leadership meeting later in the day. The all-male board was discussing upcoming changes in healthcare initiatives, specifically shifting from a "sick-care" model to a "wellness-and-prevention" model. All members were concerned about how changes in healthcare initiatives were going to impact finances and knew old solutions would not fit this new direction.

She then visited with HR leaders who voiced concern over the competition for qualified healthcare workers in the city and discussed the need to attract, hire, and keep good staff. A local university had been their main source for recruitment for years; however, their compensation plan simply could not compete with another healthcare system in the area. Ruth's organization had a retention problem as well; many promising recruits left within the first year, seeking development opportunities at other places.

In her first month, Ruth definitely had become aware of organizational culture. The hospital system, established more than 100 years ago, had rich traditions in its ways of thinking and acting. Those that attempted to challenge those traditions, change procedures, introduce new ideas, or share best practices from other hospitals or industries were immediately met with resistance.

Snapping back to the present as the executive team meeting concluded, Ruth knew her seat at the table would make all the difference for this organization.

Overview

Multiple Intelligences is a principle about honoring, valuing, and welcoming everyone to the table. It's a principle, encompassing all the previous six principles: Challenge, Relevance, Action, Novelty, Interaction, and Using Emotions, that calls us to marvel at all our differences and all our similarities. People take in information differently and demonstrate information differently. Every interaction with another human being is a sophisticated, highly complex encounter of thoughts, experiences, beliefs, strengths, and weaknesses.

Multiple Intelligences is about seeking and craving diversity, and boldly creating inclusive learning, living, and work environments. It is not about dividing people into arbitrary categories such as race, gender, age, sexual preference, analytical, creative, conservative, liberal, Western, Eastern, esoteric, practical, etc. It's about acknowledging the whole person and embracing the endless similarities and endless differences of each person on the planet.

To reiterate from a previous chapter, the brain is as unique as a fingerprint and is always changing. There are countless dimensions to every person, and when we leverage these, we have countless possibilities. Multiple Intelligences is the principle of synergy: the effects of combining elements is far greater than each individual element.

Cultures that reject Multiple Intelligences:

- always agree;
- look, think, act, and learn in similar ways;
- have leaders that mentor and develop people like them;
- address new problems with the same methods used to address old problems;
- limit possibilities for the future;
- create environments where people lack an overall sense of belonging;
- miss out on the contributions of highly talented people;
- limit themselves on current and future business opportunities;
- handicap their ability to grow their business in new markets;
- see vulnerability as a weakness;
- avoid conflict; and
- will be left behind.

The problem is we live in a world where embracing differences is not a "nice" thing to have—it's a "must" have. We are a "whole-world" society in every sense of the word. Because of our reliance on technology and a global marketplace, every person on the planet is connected in intricate ways. Even if we stay within the confines of our homes every day, the services we receive, the products we order and use, and the food we eat, connects us with people all around the world.

Cultures embracing Multiple Intelligences:

- expect healthy tension and see continuous agreement as a disadvantage;
- look, think, act, and learn in different ways, and expect that this way of being is the norm rather than the exception;
- have leaders that mentor and develop people who are not like them;
- address new problems with new methods to find new solutions;
- inspire unlimited possibilities for the future;
- create environments where people feel a sense of belonging and worth;
- capitalize on the contributions of highly talented people;
- embrace a changing marketplace and position themselves for current and future business opportunities;
- exponentially increase their chances to grow in new markets;
- see vulnerability as a core competency;
- view conflict as an opportunity to grow themselves, their relationships, and their businesses; and
- will lead the way.

In a rapidly changing world, the greatest business strategy an organization can have is to create an inclusive environment that leverages endless returns on the principle of Multiple Intelligences. In a sense, differences are what make us all the same. Our differences are our similarities. When we shift from resistance to differences to being curious about those differences, we open up a whole new world of possibility.

Reflection

- Imagine you want to be the leader in your industry. What must happen in order for you to get there?
- Describe a time when you felt like your suggestion or input was not valued. What impact did that have on you? How did it impact relationships in your life?
- Make a list of the people on your team. What are 10 similarities and what are 10 differences among them?
- Think about the people you work with. Who would you say is the most different from you?
- Describe a time when a different perspective led to a better solution.
- Rate how frequently you exhibit the following behaviors on a scale of one to four, where one is never, and four is always:

	1	2	3	4
I seek out perspectives different from my own.				
I am vulnerable with others.				
I enjoy disrupting conventional ways.				
I feel like I am valued in my organization.				

I learn about new cultures.				
I include others.				
My first response to a different idea is to stay curious.				
I become defensive when someone disagrees with me.				
I treat each person as a unique individual.				
I stand up for what is right.				
I am aware of my biases.				
I seek ways to lead change.				
I would rather hang out with people who think like me.				
I know when I become defensive.				
I adapt easily to other cultures.				

Neurology & Science

Fostering an inclusive, high-trust environment is not only the right thing to do from a human perspective, it is the right thing to do from a brain perspective. From a scientific perspective, the Multiple Intelligences principle produces results because it creates the optimal environment for the brain to operate in, and it embraces the idea that all brains are different based on life experiences and genetics.

Optimal environment

Once again, threat is the number one killer of healthy learning environments, living environments, and work environments. The greatest single thing parents, teachers, spouses, co-workers, and leaders can do is to replace high-threat cultures and interactions with high-trust cultures and interactions. We choose to create trust or create threat with every word we say, every action we take, and every belief we adopt. When the brain perceives something as threat, cortisol increases, learning and memory are compromised, emotion is triggered, activity in the prefrontal cortex is limited, and our ability to view options, think creatively, and see from other people's perspectives is narrowed.

As mentioned in previous chapters, the top threats I have encountered working with thousands of leaders for more than 20 years include social rejection, change, perceived favoritism, unrealistic or unclear expectations, risk of loss, humiliation, micromanagement, lack of meaningful work, lack of resources, and lack of honesty or trust. All result when we do not give people a choice and a voice, or do not honor their choice and voice. These threats minimize or can disappear altogether when we welcome and value people's similarities and differences.

Out of all of the threats I've mentioned, the threat of social rejection seems to be the most debilitating. When people feel shunned or rejected, the pain circuitry in their brains is activated. There is reason to believe that the brain perceives pain whether it is physical or emotional, such as the pain of not feeling valued or loved. So, in the same sense that threat to the brain is threat to the brain, pain to the brain is pain to the brain.

Consider this: if we desire for our relationships (personal or professional) to be satisfying, productive, uplifting, mutually beneficial, and healthy, why would we intentionally take action that excludes others or makes others feel rejected? When we take action that blocks a people, causing them to feel unvalued or dishonored, we create unhealthy, toxic, unproductive, and dysfunctional relationships. These relationships rarely contribute to positive results.

When we have a high-trust culture, rather than a high-threat one, people operate optimally. They bring their best ideas and best thinking to situations. They enjoy the brain-boosting power of using strengths and passions. They can meet each other on an equal playing field with the ability to see other's perspectives. Defensiveness and resistance are replaced with curiosity and understanding. What results from this type of interaction is a better individual, stronger relationships, high-functioning teamwork, and co-created solutions that offer greater possibilities.

Different brains

No two brains are alike; in fact, your brain is different now from when you began this chapter! All life experiences shape who we are, and an endless number of variables shape how we developed, who we are right now, and who we will be tomorrow.

The list is seemingly endless:

Did you grow up in poverty, wealth, or somewhere in between?

Where you physically safe?

Did you play video games inside or play creatively outside?

Did you go to private, public, or home school?

Did you have a strong family unit?

Did you have people who encouraged, invested in, and believed in you?

Did you play individual or team sports?

Did you travel often?

Did you live in different cities or countries?

Did your parents read to you?

Did you have access to a variety of experiences?

Was your home multicultural?

Did you have access to healthy foods?

Were you exposed to trauma?

Did you receive healthcare?

Did you have siblings and extended family?

Did you live in an urban, suburban, or rural area?

Were you brought up with certain spiritual values?

Were you a first-generation college student?

Were your parents or your grandparents immigrants?

—but the point is that even if you have certain things in common with one group, you most likely have twice as many differences. Even identical twins have been found to have multiple anomalies, because no two brains are alike.

Multiple Intelligences

We are also different when it comes to receiving, processing, and demonstrating learning. In the past, in the education and training world, we talked a great deal about learning style. At that time, we would give people assessments to see if they were visual, auditory, or kinesthetic. As with so many beliefs, brain research has helped us see that we are not right brain or left brain... we are whole brain. While we may lean toward visual, auditory, or kinesthetic learning, we are constantly using all our brain resources as we learn. So, when we want people to have transformational learning experiences, we want to incorporate all those learning styles, and more, all the time.

In the Using Emotion chapter, I mentioned the work of Howard Gardner, the father of the Multiple Intelligences Theory. His work not only furthered a deeper understanding of leadership but also made a monumental contribution to our understanding that all brains are different and all brains are beautiful. He shifted popular thinking from, "How smart are you?" to "How are you smart?" For centuries, we have been driven by the belief that intelligence, or "smarts," was locked into our ability to perform well at one point in time on a test (one that someone who valued that intelligence had designed and promoted). Because of the belief that intelligence could be determined by a test score, we took certain actions, and as a result, some people were included in the world of education while others were excluded. You may have been one of them; I know I was. I'm a first-generation college student, the daughter of two hard-working, loving parents. But I had no idea I was supposed to prepare for my college entrance exam. When my less-than-impressive score came back, the high school counselor called me into her office. Whether it was my score or her knowledge of my family origin, or a combination of both, she told me I wasn't "college material" and encouraged me to look at trade schools.

Gardner challenged the long-held belief that intelligence could be determined by testing. Rather, he purported that intelligence was determined by culture, specifically defining intelligence as the ability to create products and provide services valuable to the situation or culture. In leading workshops, I usually ask participants to consider the following scenarios and then determine intelligence.

- On your drive home, you round the corner to find that your house is fully engulfed in flames. The fire truck pulls up. Do you want Microsoft founder Bill Gates on the nozzle of the hose?
- You are driving alone on a long stretch of road in the desert and without any communication device. Your car breaks down. As you try to determine what is wrong with your vehicle in the scorching heat, you become severely dehydrated and pass out. One car pulls up. Who do you want behind the wheel of that car?

- You are in line at your local bank to make a transaction. Three armed people walk in, announce, "This is a robbery," and tell everyone to drop to the floor. A teller pushes the emergency button, and the police send in a team. What abilities do you want these law enforcement officers to have?
- You are living in a third-world country, and an earthquake destroys everything in your village. You are uninjured but surrounded by complete chaos. What is your most immediate need?
- You are having an emergency medical procedure. You have been prepped for surgery, given anesthetic, and are barely conscious when the surgeon is called away. The surgeon's replacement enters the room. How would you feel if horror author Stephen King entered wearing surgical attire?

What is considered "intelligence" in one situation may be the worst nightmare in another. As Gardner explains, intelligence is not a single thing that can be adequately measured by a single test. His work suggests that all individuals can have a number of independent intelligences allowing us to be strong in some areas of intelligence and weak in others. Gardner's work reveals eight different types of intelligences, defined below in no certain order, using the content from his MI Oasis website. The two I believe are most closely associated with traditional IQ and standardized testing are linguistic and logical-mathematical.

- **Linguistic Intelligence**: Sensitivity to the meaning of words, the order among words, and the sound, rhythms, inflections, and meter of words (e.g., a poet). (Sometimes called language intelligence.)

- **Logical-Mathematical Intelligence**: The capacity to conceptualize the logical relations among actions or symbols (e.g., a mathematician or a scientist). Famed psychologist Jean Piaget believed he was studying the range of intelligences, but he actually was looking at logical-mathematical intelligence.

Additionally, two more of Gardner's intelligences so closely align with the theory of Emotional Intelligence and the Using Emotion principle.

- **Intrapersonal Intelligence**: Sensitivity to one's own feelings, goals, and anxieties, and the capacity to plan and act in light of one's own traits. Intrapersonal intelligence is not particular to specific careers; rather, it is a goal for every individual in a complex modern society, where one must make consequential decisions for oneself. (Sometimes called self-intelligence.)

- **Interpersonal Intelligence**: Being able to interact effectively with others. This includes sensitivity to others' moods, feelings, temperaments and motivations (e.g., a negotiator). (Sometimes called social intelligence.)

Gardner's final four intelligences follow.

- **Spatial Intelligence**: The ability to conceptualize and manipulate large-scale spatial arrays (e.g., an airplane pilot or sailor), or more local forms of space (e.g., an architect or chess player).
- **Bodily-Kinesthetic Intelligence**: The ability to use one's whole body or its parts, such as the hands or mouth, to solve problems or create products (e.g., a dancer, a builder, or an athlete).
- **Musical Intelligence**: Sensitivity to rhythm, pitch, meter, tone, melody, and timbre. This may entail the ability to sing, play musical instruments, and/or compose music (e.g., a conductor).
- **Naturalist Intelligence**: The ability to make consequential distinctions in the world of nature as, for example, between one plant and another, or one cloud formation and another (e.g., a taxonomist). (Sometimes called nature intelligence.)

Now look back at one of the previous scenarios—the house fire, the need for roadside assistance, the earthquake, the bank robbery, or the impending surgery. None implies only one intelligence; rather, each problem demands a blend of intelligences. And, the worth of the intelligence is defined by the nature of the need. The signature intelligence needed for becoming a national chess champion may be different from the one needed to become the starting point guard for a professional basketball team. And that's OK. Both are equally valuable signature intelligences that depend on the need.

If anything, brain research and intelligences challenge us to marvel at the beauty, mystery, and complexity of the human brain. We simply must move past egocentric, limiting beliefs that pigeon-hole humans into categories. Instead, our focus must be on creating the optimal environment for the brain to thrive. Much like the plant mentioned earlier, when placed in the right environment, the brain flourishes. We have to appreciate all our differences and similarities, and look for ways we can use them to become our best selves, both individually and collectively.

Application

One of my favorite movies is "The Matrix." In the infamous pill scene, Neo (played by Keanu Reeves) must make a choice that will change his life forever. With crackling thunder and lightning in the background, Morpheus (Laurence Fishburne) observes that Neo is confused, like Alice tumbling down a rabbit hole into wonderland. Morpheus tells Neo that he is a slave because he lives in a world that has blinded him from the truth. This bondage is a prison of the mind. Morpheus offers Neo a blue pill and a red pill. If he takes the blue pill, he will go on with life as usual. If he takes the red pill, his eyes will be open and his life will never be the same.

Once you know, you can't unknow. Many of the discoveries we make in applying the principle of Multiple Intelligences are convicting and painful. Many of us don't want to hear and discover that we have bias, and it has most likely sabotaged our success to some degree and negatively impacted other people. We don't want to hear that a person's zip code may determine how long a person lives and her quality of life, due to exposure to harm, negative influences, a poor diet, or lack of access to healthcare. Most people are content with taking the blue pill. It is painful to take the red pill.

But for those who are willing to take the red pill, who look in the mirror, do the hard work, and have the courage to make the necessary changes, they will change the world.

Unconscious bias

Unconscious bias is real, and if you are human, you have it. Unconscious, or implicit, bias is the opposite of conscious (explicit) bias. Unconscious bias doesn't mean a person deliberately or knowingly holds predispositions against groups of people or experiences. After all, it is bias that we are not consciously aware of. Therefore, unless we work to define and see our unconscious bias, we can live a lifetime never knowing its impact on our own success and that of others.

According to the Kirwan Institute for the Study of Race and Ethnicity at The Ohio State University, unconscious bias impacts our understanding, our actions, and our decisions because of the attitudes or stereotypes we unknowingly hold. These biases can be based on an endless number of factors and can be directed toward those outside or within our "like group." According to the Institute, unconscious bias is the cumulative result of the experiences, messages, beliefs, and influences we are exposed to throughout life. A few facts about unconscious biases follow.

- They are part of the human experience. Everyone has them—yes, everyone. Unconscious (implicit) bias has been the topic of thousands of studies in the last 10 years which conclusively show that if you are a living, breathing human, you have bias.

- They are not always a bad thing. For example, say you are in a dark parking lot alone at night, and you see someone lurking in the shadows with a weapon. Your associations may save your life.

- They are processed very quickly. We believe 99% of all learning is unconscious; some scientists predict we may be hit with 11 million bits of information per second. But, our brain processing time is limited and can only process about 40 bits of information per second.

- They are deeply ingrained and difficult to unlearn. A fish is not consciously aware of the water because it has always been a part of its experience. In much the same way, we are not aware of our bias because it, too, has always been a part of our experience.

- They limit our individual and collective growth. Because of unconscious bias, we misread and therefore overlook the value and potential in ourselves, in others, in situations, and in opportunities. So we suffer, as do our relationships, successes, and endeavors.

While we can't eliminate unconscious bias, we can seek ways to minimize its negative consequences. A few ideas for reducing the impact of unconscious bias are:

- Educate yourself and others about unconscious bias. Improvement begins the moment we realize such a phenomenon exists.
- Raise awareness about the negative impact unconscious bias can have. Help others discover how it may impact how they react and respond to people, situations, and opportunities.
- Become increasingly self-aware. Start with gathering data on yourself. Where might you need increased awareness of how bias may be showing up in your life and relationships?
- Gather data about the organization in which you operate. What groups are most often impacted? What, where, and how is the impact costing those involved?
- Stay curious and always be eager to learn about others, particularly those whose lives, views, backgrounds, and experiences are different from your own.

- Make an intentional effort to expand your circle of input. Actively seek opportunities to build diverse teams or gather feedback from diverse sources.
- Keep an open mind for new role models. When we study and learn from people who violate the stereotype or perception we may initially hold, we expand our thinking, have a new experience, and shift our beliefs.
- Recognize the power of real stories. When we hear a compelling story, our brains release oxytocin, the same chemical released when our brains feel empathy. If you are looking to challenge biases, share a powerful story or read the biographies of those who are different from you.
- Promote awareness and publicity of people or projects that encourage positive images of specific groups.
- Look for multiple ways to integrate conversations around strengths, differences, inclusion, and bias into your day-to-day business. Talk about it in meetings, incorporate it into learning materials and presentations, etc.
- Have a new experience. Let's return for a moment to the model I use in coaching. We must remember that our reality is the result of our actions, feelings, beliefs, and experiences. So if we want to adopt new beliefs, which drive our feelings, actions, and results, we must have new experiences.

Experiences

Mechanical engineer and writer Yassmin Abdel-Magied offers a powerful TED talk, "What does my headscarf mean to you?" Her insightful words point to how frequently we misread people because of unconscious bias and what it costs not only individuals, but the world in general. She not only helps us better see the problem, but she offers practical steps we can take for moving past it. One of her suggestions is to actively seek new experiences to challenge our limiting beliefs. She recommends that we purposely interact with a community of people different from ourselves or to mentor someone who, at first glance, may seem nothing like us. Her suggestions work because when we have a new experience, we shift our beliefs, thoughts, and stories. We must be willing to step outside of what is comfortable and conventional and have new experiences.

Inclusive leadership

Never before has the need to have new experiences and embrace diversity been so critical to business and leadership. With increasing technology and rapidly rising consumer demands, embracing diversity and inclusion is essential to business survival. A recent study by the financial company Deloitte alerts us to critical economic trends and argues for inclusive leadership. Their research reveals four global mega-trends reshaping the environment and influencing business priorities.

- Diversity of markets—The growing middle class is the consumer of the future.
- Diversity of customers—The customer expects personalization and a voice.
- Diversity of ideas—Business is in a race for diverse thinking and innovation.
- Diversity of talent—The workforces of today and tomorrow seek to be treated as individuals, they want to grow themselves and their career, and they want purpose as much as a paycheck.

According to Deloitte, these trends demand inclusive leadership, a capability that reflects six signature traits:

- **Commitment**: Inclusive leaders are dedicated to inclusion and diversity not only because it's good for business, productivity, and profits, but because it first and foremost aligns with their values.
- **Courage**: Inclusive leaders must be brave enough to speak up, challenge convention, and disrupt the status quo. They must be humble about their strengths and weaknesses while at the same time stand their ground in advancing a topic that triggers resistance.
- **Cognizance of bias**: Inclusive leaders know about conscious and unconscious bias both personally and organizationally. They take an active role in increasing their own self-awareness and in driving the organization to identify and better manage bias by implementing best-practice strategies.

- **Curiosity**: Inclusive leaders maintain an open mind, a willingness to learn and be coachable, a desire to withhold judgment, and the ability to meet people where they are. They strive not to change but to understand an ever-increasing global workforce and marketplace.
- **Culturally intelligent**: Inclusive leaders may have IQ and EQ, (Emotional Intelligence) but they must also have CQ (cultural intelligence). Culturally intelligence leaders avoid an egocentric approach to other cultures. They manage themselves well in ambiguous, uncertain, and unclear situations.
- **Collaborative**: Inclusive leaders are committed to empowering individuals and creating environments where individuals are motivated and feel safe to share their opinions and ideas. They do not have to be convinced that the whole is greater than the sum of the parts. They already know this and seek ways to promote collaboration and diversity of thought.

These six signature traits support a CRANIUM culture. For leaders to truly live by these traits, they must be mindful of creating an inclusive culture. The CRANIUM principles provide the necessary environment for inclusive leadership to truly take shape and transform businesses so they are prepared to address the four changing trends of markets, customers, ideas, and talent. The following is a review of the CRANIUM principles, featuring specific ways each is critical for inclusive leadership.

Challenge minimizes threat and increases trust. It provides an environment in which people feel safe in taking risks and challenging traditions and social norms. Individuals must have a sense of security and belonging before they will step outside their comfort zone, be vulnerable with one another, and openly express their opinions and ideas. They must feel supported if they are to have the courage to challenge norms and confront situations that need to be addressed. They must operate in a high-trust culture if they are to be curious, stay in place of not knowing, and seek to understand instead of feeling like they always need to know the answer. High trust and low threat are essential environments for people to be confident in learning about other cultures and collaborating with people whose ideas differ from their own.

Relevance is about vision and values, keeping purpose front-and-center, and building on individual strengths. This principle is critical to the commitment trait of inclusive leaders. They must be clear on the vision and values of the organization as well as for themselves as individuals. They must also be able to take those visions and values one step further and connect the two to each individual's vision and values. It is essential that leaders remain clear on how Multiple Intelligences is good for the business, for each individual employee, and for themselves personally. Relevance is also about seeking out and building on strengths, a requirement for being culturally intelligent and for promoting collaboration.

Action works with the brain's limitations as much as with its endless capabilities. Inclusive leaders tune into the unique needs and limitations of each individual; they adapt processes and schedules to what works best for each one, and honor an individual's need to integrate work and life in a healthy way.

Novelty is about innovation, diverse thinking, and creativity. It is a natural outcome when leaders are successful in fostering inclusive cultures. Novelty happens when people feel safe to challenge and think differently, have the courage to stand up against what is no longer working and advocate for what is right, and collaborate with people whose ideas and approaches may be vastly different from their own. Above all, novelty happens in the face of humility; people must be able to put aside their need to be right and be the superhero with the one right answer. Inclusive leadership keeps an open mind for learning. They are less concerned about who gets the credit and more concerned about finding a better solution. They don't have to be the ones to take the ball across the goal line; they desire to be a part of the team that gets the ball to the goal line.

Interaction gives people a choice and voice, engaging them in as many ways as possible to give others a sense of ownership in the outcome. Inclusive leadership must fully rely on this principle. It requires that leaders stay in a place of "power with" rather than "power over" by staying curious, being eager to learn and grow, and remaining coachable. They actively seek the voice and input of others who have thoughts different from their own. Because they seek commitment over compliance, seek "ask" rather than "tell," and seek to understand rather than respond, inclusive leaders are confident and effective in working with other cultures and promoting a spirit of collaboration.

Using Emotion is about capitalizing on the emotional brain, never losing sight that it is more emotional than logical. If we truly want people to engage and transform, we must put feeling first, because that's how our equipment works. Inclusive leadership requires that leaders never lose sight of the power of emotion. All six traits—commitment, courage, cognizance of bias, curiosity, cultural intelligence, and collaboration—have a common denominator: that leaders never forget the human element.

People are emotional individuals who happen to think, and emotions run the show. Inclusive leaders are ever-mindful that regardless of the business or industry they are in, the process improvement they are trying to drive, or the change they strive to lead, they are first and foremost dealing with human beings. People run on emotion.

Incorporating these principles and striving for an inclusive culture is not only the right *humanitarian* thing to do; it's the right *business* thing to do.

Those businesses already on their way to embracing Multiple Intelligences won't be rattled by trends impacting the workplace. Their leaders are championing inclusive cultures. Their experiences lead them to adopt the driving belief that the greatest resource they have is their people. They know that their success in getting the business part right hinges on their ability to get the people part right.

Potential is unlocked, and possibilities are unleashed, when we operate by the principle of Multiple Intelligences. This principle honors all our differences and all our similarities. Differences show up in a thousand ways of learning, living, thinking, and communicating—and your way of being and intelligence does not devalue mine. We can agree; that's OK, because everyone can win. But we don't always have to agree, and that's OK; again, everyone can win. We don't have to be threatened by differences, and we don't have to fully understand them to appreciate them. They are, in fact, our greatest asset and our greatest competitive advantage if we choose to see them as such.

When we can shift our belief and seek out and appreciate all that makes us different and all that makes us the same, we become better individuals. We emerge as part of organizations that are more culturally, environmentally, and socially responsible, equipped to stay wildly profitable in a rapidly changing marketplace. Above all, when we intentionally live out the principle of Multiple Intelligences, we have a voice in creating a healthier, happier, and safer planet for generations to come.

Conclusion

Our brains are the most marvelous, complex, and awe-inspiring technology in all of history. That three-pound bad boy in our head stands between where we are now and accomplishing what seems impossible. It is the source of "no matter what" moments, like climbing Mt. Everest or enduring grueling, unjust moments in life. It also is the source of "freak show" moments, like the ones that end up trending on social media.

When we apply what we know about the brain, we make things easier. We can accomplish more, make smarter decisions, live out our better selves, develop those around us, and care for things that matter. When we do not apply our knowledge of the brain's abilities, we make things harder. We add unnecessary stress, live in conflict, hold ourselves and others back from reaching full potential, and ignore or harm the things that truly matter. In the end, it's our choice: we can use what we know to create positive unforgettables or ignore what we know to create negative unforgettables.

I am proud to live in a small community with a history rich in farming. Listen to farmers talk, and you will quickly begin to appreciate the importance of respecting universal laws. Farming is one profession that encounters innumerable uncontrollables. Farmers simply have no control over weather patterns, rainfall, drought, or the invasion of unexpected pests. In addition, farmers have no control over certain universal laws. For example, if a farmer wants to grow corn, that farmer must plant corn. If a farmer wants to harvest during one season, that farmer must plant in the appropriate season for that crop to be harvested. Farmers can either choose to battle, argue, and work against the uncontrollables and universal laws, or they can opt to work with the uncontrollables and universal laws. The latter typically yields better results and a longer life for farmers.

As leaders seeking to develop ourselves and those around us, we can learn a few lessons from farmers. We can choose to focus on the uncontrollables, such as the unpredictability of human behavior, and we can stay in a reactive mode when faced with the increasing complexities that come with a rapidly changing, competitive world. Or, we can choose to focus on the universal truths, the unchanging, guiding principles of how the brain works best. When we focus on the seven CRANIUM principles, we create the optimal environment for the best results, regardless of the change, the subject, or the situation.

First, we must honor Challenge. If we want to operate at our best, and if we want those we seek to influence to operate at their best, we simply must build trust and minimize threat. This is perhaps the most important of the principles. The brain's performance, and even our health, is dramatically impacted by threat and high-threat environments. So, if we want to gain unforgettable results like collaboration, cooperation, innovation, creativity, and self-control, we will intentionally and purposefully seek ways to challenge ourselves and others in a high-trust environment. Sure, we can continue leading, living, and teaching with threat-producing tactics like humiliation, micromanagement, favoritism, and posturing. But if we make that choice, we forfeit the right to blame, complain, criticize, or point fingers when we don't see results.

The second principle we must recognize is Relevance. The human brain performs best when it is motivated by a compelling "why" and purpose. I often ask people attending my workshops to think of a time when they were successful in achieving a personal or professional goal. Typical responses include, "I lost 40 pounds last year;" "I traveled to Europe;" and "I took my family to five different national parks over the summer."

When asked why they thought they were successful in achieving those goals, as opposed to others they had set in their lives but had not accomplished, I often hear, "Because

Conclusion

I was sick and tired of feeling tired;" "I have wanted to travel to another country my entire life;" and "My kids are growing up so fast, and I wanted to experience that with them." But I don't hear people say, "I lost weight because my boss told me I needed to, so I got up at 5 a.m. every morning to go to the gym before work."

Rather, each person offers a motivating, inspiring "why." Purpose and meaning were built on their inner desires. Of all the questions we ask, the most important may be, "So what matters to you?" If we fail to honor relevance, we may gain compliance, but we will never achieve commitment.

Action is the principle in direct opposition to our cultural ADD. We shouldn't be surprised when we suffer natural consequences because of the choices we either do, or do not, make. If the car is low on fuel and we don't stop at the gas station, there is a natural consequence—a long walk home. If we are pulled over for exceeding the speed limit in a school zone, there is a natural consequence—a big ticket to pay. If we fail to take the time to invest in the important relationships in our lives, there is a natural consequence—isolation. If we show up for work late every day, there is a natural consequence—unemployed.

The same is true for the most amazing piece of equipment on the planet. I'm in awe of the capacity of the marvelously complex human brain. However, its limitations must be respected, or there will be natural consequences. If we constantly multitask, there are natural consequences—

tasks get done, but not correctly. If we don't ensure that we have enough sleep, push harder in times of stress, work longer at the expense of healthy eating and exercise, or fail to repair the brain when it is not working properly, there are natural consequences--illness. Like the other CRANIUM principles, the Action principle helps us see the importance of working with, rather than against, how the brain works best. When we embrace that fact, we live happier, healthier, and longer. When we ignore that fact, we suffer natural consequences.

Novelty and its companions—innovation and creativity—are prized commodities in a rapidly changing world where competition is fierce. However, more attention is given to the result than to the conditions needed to promote the result. Innovation and creativity imply risk, and most organizations, already operating in threat, aren't equipped to create a safe environment for innovation and creativity to grow. Novelty requires leveraging strengths, and most organizations still approach development from a deficit-closing rather than a strengths-building approach. Novelty craves change, a requirement that requires clarity; unfortunately, most organizations lack the clear communication that helps reduce the resistance change often stirs up. Novelty depends on collaboration, and most organizations still operate as a group of people working as individuals rather than individuals working together as a group. However, those who do create an optimal environment in which novelty can thrive will leave the competition far behind and change the world.

Tell them, they comply. Involve them, they commit. When we violate this belief, we violate the important principle of Interaction. If we want to foster engagement, ownership, and accountability, we must involve rather than tell. If we want the people around us to truly develop, discover the best solutions, and become mature problem-solvers, we must first facilitate discovery. If we want to create cultures where everyone, regardless of title, can engage in respectful and fearless conversations about performance improvement, we must move away from "boss" and move toward "coach." We must venture away from solving problems, giving orders, and sharing advice to meeting people where they are in a way that promotes discovery, increased awareness, and new learning.

The sixth principle involves Using Emotion. If we want to lead change, enhance learning, and motivate development, we simply must engage emotion. Our emotions are contagious; they can propel us forward and build commitment and engagement, or make us sick, both figuratively and literally. The power of emotion can drive us to greatness or drive us to the grave.

We simply cannot ignore emotion, the human element, as we seek to accomplish tasks and achieve results. Doing so only makes progress slower and creates greater stress and conflict.

Finally, every brain wants to feel welcomed and included to some extent. Every brain has value to add.

Every brain has limitations, biases, and blind spots. And every brain is wildly unique. An inclusive environment is one which quickly goes beyond the old notions of gender, race, and age, to the belief that different perspectives produce better results. These results may not be quicker or easier to attain, but they are always better. An inclusive environment is one in which all our differences and all our similarities are acknowledged and honored, allowing us to fully bring our multiple perspectives to achieve better results.

It comes down to this: getting the results we want for ourselves, our schools, our workplaces, and our nation is really not complicated at all. We simply have to create cultures that are aligned with how the brain naturally works best. It doesn't have to be hard. Trust the principles, and enjoy unforgettable rewards.

Resources

Acuff, John. Start: Punch Fear in the Face, Escape Average, and Do Work That Matters. Ramsey Press, 2013.

Cochran, Veronica. L.I.F.E. Concepts; www.life-concepts.org. Accessed 27 Aug 2018.

Medina, John. Brain Rules: 12 Principles for Surviving and Thriving at Work, Home, and School. Pear Press, 2008.

D'Argembeau, Arnaud; Ruby, Perinne; Collette, Fabienne; Degueldre, Christian; Balteau, Evelyne; Luxen, André; Maquet, Pierre; Salmon, Eric. "Distinct regional of the medial prefrontal cortex are associated with self-referential processing and perspective taking." Journal of Cognitive Neuroscience. 2007; 19 (6): 935-944.

Kross, Ethan; Berman, Marc G.; Mischel, Walter; Smith, Edward E.; Wager, Tor D. "Social rejection shares somatosensory representations with physical pain." Proceedings of the National Academy of Sciences. 2011; 108 (15): 6270-6275. https://doi.org/10.1073/pnas.1102693108

Heller, Joseph. Catch-22. Simon & Schuster, 1961.

Jensen, Eric. Teaching with Poverty in Mind: What Being Poor Does to Kids' Brains and What Schools Can Do About It. Association for Supervision & Curriculum Development, 2009.

Covey, Stephen M.R. The Speed of Trust: The One Thing That Changes Everything. Free Press, 2008.

Gallup. How Millennials Want to Work and Live. 2016. www.gallup.com. Accessed 27 Aug 2018.

LeDoux, Joseph. Anxious: Using the Brain to Understand and Treat Fear and Anxiety. Penguin Books, 2016.

Rock, David. Quiet Leadership: Six Steps to Transforming Performance at Work. HarperBusiness, 2007.

Hebb, D. O. The Organization of Behavior: A Neuropsychological Theory. John Wiley & Sons, Inc., 1949.

Beilock, Sian. Choke: What the Secrets of the Brain Reveal About Getting It Right When You Have To. Free Press, 2010.

Jensen, Eric P. Fierce Teaching: Purpose, Passion, and What Matters Most. Corwin, 2009.

Rock, David. "SCARF: A Brain-Based Model for Collaborating with and Influencing Others." Neuroleadership Institute Journal. 2008: (1).

Collins, Jim. Good to Great: Why Some Companies Make the Leap... and Others Don't. HarperBusiness, 2001.

Resources

Buckingham, Marcus; Clifton, Donald O. Now, Discover Your Strengths. Gallup Press, 2001.

Gallup. State of the American Workplace, 2017. www.gallup.com. Accessed 27 Aug 2018.

Rock, David. Your Brain at Work: Strategies for Overcoming Distraction, Regaining Focus, and Working Smarter All Day Long. HarperBusiness, 2009.

Amen, Daniel G. Making a Good Brain Great. Three Rivers Press, 2005.

Mark, Gloria; Gudith, Daniela; Klocke, Ulrich. "The Cost of Interrupted Work: More Speed and Stress." Proceedings of the SIGCHI Conference on Human Factors in Computing Systems. https://www.ics.uci.edu/~gmark/chi08-mark.pdf. Accessed 27 Aug 2018.

American Psychological Association. "Multitasking: Switching Costs." https://www.apa.org/research/action/multitask.aspx. Accessed 27 Aug 2018.

Johnson, Steve Berlin. "Emerging Technology: How to Cut Through the Info Blitz and Actually Get Some Work Done." Discover Magazine. 22 Nov 2005. http://discovermagazine.com/2005/nov/emerging-technology/

Foerde, Karin; Knowlton, Barbara J.; Poldrack, Russell A. "Modulation of Competing Memory Systems by Distraction." Proceedings of the National Academy of Sciences of the United States of America. 2006: 103 (31) 11778-83. https://doi.org/10.1073/pnas.0602659103.

National Sleep Foundation. "National Sleep Foundation Recommends New Sleep Times." 2 Feb 2015.

https://sleepfoundation.org/press-release/national-sleep-foundation-recommends-new-sleep-times

Centers for Disease Control and Prevention. "Drowsy Driving: Asleep at the Wheel." 7 Nov 2017. https://www.cdc.gov/features/dsdrowsydriving/index.html

Pink, Daniel. When: The Scientific Secrets of Perfect Timing. Riverhead Books, 2018.

Rosch, Paul J. "The Quandry of Job Stress Compensation." Health and Stress: The Newsletter of the American Institute of Stress. 2001: Issue 1, 1.

Rahe, Richard H.; Mahan Jr., JL; Arthur, RJ. "Prediction of near-future health change from subjects' preceding life changes." Journal of Psychosomatic Research. 1970: 14 (4) 401-406.

Swenson, Richard A. Margin: Restoring Emotional, Physical, Financial, and Time Reserves to Overloaded Lives. Navpress, 1992.

The Dana Foundation. "Brain Awareness Week 2009: Seven Brain Facts for Seven Days." https://www.dana.org/Publications/Details.aspx?id=43492. Accessed 27 Aug 2018.

Centers for Disease Control and Prevention. "CDC Report: Mental Illness Surveillance Among Adults in the United States," 2 Dec 2011. https://www.cdc.gov/mentalhealthsurveillance/fact_sheet.html

Rubin, Gretchen. Better than Before: What I Learned about Making and Breaking Habits – To Sleep More, Quit Sugar, Procrastinate Less, and Generally Build a Happier

Resources

Life. Broadway Books, 2015.

Shekerjian, Denise. Uncommon Genius How Great Ideas Are Born: Tracing the Creative Impulse of 40 Winners of the MacArthur Award. Penguin Books, 1991.

Burchard, Brendon. High Performance Habits: How Extraordinary People Become That Way. Hay House Inc., 2017.

Medina, John. Brain Rules: 12 Principles for Surviving and Thriving at Work, Home, and School. Pear Press, 2008.

Bunzeck, Nico; Düzel, Emrah. "Absolute Coding of Stimulus Novelty in the Human Substantia Nigra/VTA." Neuron. 2006: 51 (3) 369-379.

Reavis, George. The Animal School. Crystal Springs Books, 1999.

Rath, Tom and Barry Conchie. Strengths Based Leadership: Great Leaders, Teams, and Why People Follow. Gallup Press, 2008.

Weihenmayer, Erik. "A Blind Ascent: Summiting Everest Without Sight." Outdoor. 14 May 2012. https://www.outsideonline.com/1909131/blind-ascent-summiting-everest-without-sight

Centers for Disease Control and Prevention. "Adult Obesity Facts." 12 June 2018. https://www.cdc.gov/obesity/data/adult.html

Project: Time Off. "State of American Vacation 2018." https://projecttimeoff.com/wp-content/uploads/2018/05/StateofAmericanVacation2018.pdf. Accessed 27 Aug 2018.

Gallup. "State of the American Workplace," Feb 2017. https://news.gallup.com/reports/178514/state-american-workplace.aspx. Accessed 27 Aug 2018.

Centers for Disease Control and Prevention. "1 in 3 Adults Don't Get Enough Sleep," 18 Feb 2016. https://www.cdc.gov/media/releases/2016/p0215-enough-sleep.html

Centers for Disease Control and Prevention. "CDC Report: Mental Illness Surveillance Among Adults in the United States." 2 Dec 2011. https://www.cdc.gov/mentalhealthsurveillance/fact_sheet.html

Rubin, Gretchen. Better than Before: What I Learned about Making and Breaking Habits – To Sleep More, Quit Sugar, Procrastinate Less, and Generally Build a Happier Life. Broadway Books, 2015.

Shekerjian, Denise. Uncommon Genius How Great Ideas Are Born: Tracing the Creative Impulse of 40 Winners of the MacArthur Award. Penguin Books, 1991.

Medina, John. Brain Rules: 12 Principles for Surviving and Thriving at Work, Home, and School. Pear Press, 2008.

Paul, Richard; Paul, Linda. The Art of Socratic Questioning. The Foundation for Critical Thinking. 2007. https://www.criticalthinking.org/store/get_file.php?inventories_id=231&inventories_files_id=374. Accessed 27 Aug 2018.

http://bloomstaxonomy.org

Kotter, John P; Cohen, Dan S. The Heart of Change: Real-Life Stories of How People Change Their

Resources

Organizations. John P. Kotter and Deloitte Consulting, LLC, 2002.

Jensen, Eric P. Fierce Teaching: Purpose, Passion, and What Matters Most. Corwin, 2009.

Almendrala, Anna. "Weight Watchers More Successful Than Self-Help Approach, Study Finds." 15 Oct 2013. https://www.huffingtonpost.com/2013/10/15/weight-watchers-study-self-help_n_4099023.html

Eyre, Linda; Eyre, Richard. Teaching Your Children Responsibility. Fireside Books, 1982.

Patterson, Kerry; Grenny, Joseph; McMillan, Ron; Switzler, Al. Crucial Conversations: Tools for Talking When Stakes are High. McGraw-Hill, 2012.

Craine, Thomas G.. The Heart of Coaching: Using Transformational Coaching to Create a High-Performance Coaching Culture. 2nd Edition. 2002

International Coach Federation. https://coachfederation.org.

Gallup. "How Millennials Want to Work and Live." 2016 https://www.gallup.com/workplace/238073/millennials-work-live.aspx

Gallup. How Millennials Want to Work and Live. 2016. www.gallup.com. Accessed 27 Aug 2018.

Studer, Quint. The Magic of Rounding. http://isosupport.com/wp-content/uploads/2015/05/2005_Nov_The-Magic-of-Rounding.pdf. 2005

Burton, Kate. Coaching with NLP for Dummies. Wiley, 2011.

Heath, Chip; Heath, Dan. Switch: How to Change Things When Change is Hard. Broadway Books, 2010.

Achor, Shawn. The Happiness Advantage: The Seven Principles of Positive Psychology That Fuel Success and Performance at Work. Crown Business, 2010.

LeDoux, Joseph. The Emotional Brain: The Mysterious Underpinnings of Emotional Life. Touchstone, 1998.

Beilock, Sian. Choke: What the Secrets of the Brain Reveal About Getting It Right When You Have To. Free Press, 2010.

Hanson, Rick. "Take in the Good." http://www.rickhanson.net/take-in-the-good/. Accessed 27 Aug 2018.

Cleveland Clinic. "Wanna Give? This is Your Brain on a 'Helper's High.'" 15 Nov 2016. https://health.clevelandclinic.org/tag/helpers-high/

Buckingham, Marcus; Clifton, Donald O. Now, Discover Your Strengths. Gallup Press, 2001.

Quillien, Jenny. Clever Digs: How Workspaces Can Enable Thought. Culicidae Press LLC, 2012.

VIA Institute on Character. https://www.viacharacter.org/www/. Accessed 27 Aug 2018.

Gardner, Howard. Multiple Intelligences: The Theory in Practice. BasicBooks, 1993.

Goleman, Daniel. Emotional Intelligence: Why It Can Matter More than IQ. Bantam Books, 1995.

Goleman, Daniel; Boyatzis, Richard; McKee, Annie. Primal Leadership: Unleashing the Power of Emotional Intelligence. Harvard Business Review Press, 2013.

Resources

Harper Lee. To Kill a Mockingbird. Lippincott, 1960.

Gardner, Howard. Multiple Intelligences: The Theory in Practice. BasicBooks, 1993.

Weir, Kirsten. "The Pain of Social Rejection." 2012: 43 (4) 50. http://www.apa.org/monitor/2012/04/rejection.aspx

Kirwan Institute for the Study of Race and Ethnicity. "Understanding Implicit Bias." 2015. http://kirwaninstitute.osu.edu/research/understanding-implicit-bias/. Accessed 27 Aug 2018.

MI Oasis. http://multipleintelligencesoasis.org/. Accessed 27 Aug 2018.

Abdel-Magied, Yassmin. "What Does My Headscarf Mean to You?" TEDxSouthBank, Dec 2014. https://www.ted.com/talks/yassmin_abdel_magied_what_does_my_headscarf_mean_to_you. Accessed 27 Aug 2018.

Dillon, Bernadette; Bourke, Juliet. The Six Signature Traits of Inclusive Leadership: Thriving in a Diverse New World. Deloitte University Press, 2015.

Crane, Thomas G. The Heart of Coaching: Using Transformational Coaching to Create a High-Performance Coaching Culture. FTA Press, 2002.